TAEGEUK:
the NEW FORMS
of Tae Kwon Do

by Pu Gill Gwon

Editor: Michael Lee
Graphic Design: Karen Massad

Cover Photo: Mario Prado
Art Production: Junko N. Sadjadpour

D0027027

©1984 Ohara Publications,Inc.
All rights reserved
Printed in the United States of America
Library of Congress Catalog Card Number: 83-063602
ISBN 0-89750-097-0

Sixteenth printing 1999

OHARA PUBLICATIONS, INCORPORATED
SANTA CLARITA, CALIFORNIA

WARNING

Dedication

This book is dedicated to all martial artists, and most especially to Chul and Yise Gwon.

I would like to take the opportunity of extending my heartiest congratulations to Master Pu Gill Gwon on the publication of his Taegeuk forms textbook.

Although tae kwon do was originated in Korea two thousand years ago, it is now the duty and privilege of all tae kwon do students to join in our common effort to make it a universal sport.

Demand for qualified tae kwon do textbooks is rising, especially after the recognition of the World Tae Kwon Do Federation by the International Olympic Committee. I am sure Mr. Gwon's publication will serve greatly to help students at all levels.

I am proud to recommend this publication because Mr. Gwon speaks not only from his long experience and technical knowledge, but also with the authority of the World Tae Kwon Do Federation.

Sincerely,

Un Yong Kim
President,
The World Tae Kwon Do Federation

About the Author

Pu Gill Gwon was born near Seoul, Korea. When he was a child, he moved with his family to Pusan, Korea, and while in school there, learned Western-style boxing. For young Pu Gill Gwon, his work in the boxing ring started him on the road to martial arts success. He won the Junior Boxing Championships in his tournament class, and in 1953, he met his first Korean martial arts instructor, Ha Dae Young, and began the study of tae kwon do. From there, he branched out into the study of judo with Chang Hang Je.

In 1954, Pu Gill Gwon joined the Korean Navy's underwater demolition team. His superb physique, excellent health and agility, developed from a religiously dedicated pursuit of the martial arts, saw him through the difficult training so well that he advanced from student to instructor and was assigned to the Korean Navy intelligence section in 1959. Gwon regards his tours as a teacher in the intelligence division as probably the most difficult and hazardous of his life.

In 1967, he joined the International Tae Kwon Do Federation. Pu Gill Gwon visited the United States in 1971 to demonstrate his techniques, including his dynamic breaking techniques, at various exhibitions. The public response was so enthusiastic that he stayed on and opened his first dojang in Baltimore, Maryland.

Today, Pu Gill Gwon has eight schools in various locations in the United States. He attributes the popularity of his classes to the dedication of his students.

The art of dynamic breaking, as developed by Pu Gill Gwon, has brought standing ovations across the country, beginning in 1975 at the Martial Arts Exhibition in Chicago promoted by Jim Jones.

Pu Gill Gwon has written for Ohara Publications *The Dynamic Art of Breaking,* published in 1977, *Skill in Counterattacks,* published in 1979, and *Basic Training for Kicking,* published in 1981, and had a feature role in the movie *Desperate Targets.*

He is currently president of the Korean Tae Kwon Do Association in the United States.

Philosophy
of the Forms

The Taegeuk forms are essentially paradigms of the tae kwon do system of martial arts. They contain the basic physical movements which must be mastered to become proficient in this discipline. In addition, they also contain the thoughts which accompany the practice of tae kwon do, and from which tae kwon do draws much of its social and humanistic worth.

All systems of self-defense inevitably lead the thoughtful practitioner to considerations of death, and consequently to considerations of the meaning of life; and this is why Taegeuk is inextricably bound to the ideas found in one of the noblest documents in the Orient addressing the meaning of life—the *Jooyeok,* the *Book of Changes.*

The *Book of Changes* is an ancient work composed by several Chinese sages over a period spanning many hundreds of years. It elaborates a theory in which the phenomemon of constant, shifting change, which is the human condition, is shown to possess a moral harmony. It analyzes the process in which two opposing metaphysical forces called *um* and *yang* (the Korean names for yin and yang) combine to generate new combinations; and this is seen as the conceptual mechanism which propitiates life and the universe.

Fuh Hi, the original author of the *Book of Changes,* who lived in the 13th century B.C., identified eight subsequent combinations derived from the two primal forces, um and yang. He named them, and arranged them in a circle to illustrate their harmonious relationships, and designated the character of each. These eight concepts, he showed, manifest themselves in all things, including our human destiny.

Keon, the first, is a concept which is pure um. It is the unbridled creative force associated with heaven and light. *Tae,* the second, is the concept of joy. The third, *ri,* means fire and the sun, and it is interpreted as the creative passion. *Jin,* the fourth, symbolizes thunder, suggesting courage in the face of danger. *Seon,* the fifth, symbolizes wind, sometimes gentle, sometimes forceful. *Gam,* the sixth, means water, and the characteristics of constancy and flow. *Gan,* the seventh, means "top stop," suggesting the wisdom of knowing where and when to stop.

KEON
乾
1

TAE
兌
2

SEON
巽
5

RI
離
3

GAM
坎
6

GAN
艮
7

JIN
震
4

GON
坤
8

Gon, the eighth, and keon, the first, are the keys to understanding the dialectics of the great circle. Gon is a concept which is pure yang. Opposite keon, it symbolizes the yielding earth, which provides the substance and the limitations through which keon passes. The results are forms—forms, without which the universe is nothingness—physical manifestations infused with some measure of the creative force, the potential to rise to a higher place on the chain of being.

In gon is realized the nature of keon; and in keon, the nature of gon. Each defines the other in the paradox from which creation itself is congealed into reality, and into time.

The eight Taegeuk forms are intended for the mental as well as the physical training of tae kwon do practitioners, combining as it does, basic movements with philosophical thoughts. The student, in preparing himself for advancement, is urged to maintain a good balance in his own mind between his martial skills and the traditional values of tae kwon do.

Preface

The forms in this book are the basic underlayment of tae kwon do. Tae kwon do represents an Oriental Philosophical view of the world, the cosmos, and life. Taegeuk is written in Chinese as (太極). "Tae (太)" means bigness, and "geuk (極)" means eternity. Thus, speaking philosophically, Taegeuk has neither the limitations of space nor time. Nevertheless, everything in tae kwon do comes from Taegeuk.

The thoughts contained in Taegeuk are the principal teachings of the *Jooyeok, Book of Changes,* which is one of the primary statements of Oriental philosophy. Out of the *Book of Changes* come eight major branches of thought, each of which is named by a Chinese character. Taegeuk forms one through eight are based on these thoughts. In practicing these forms, you must move your body in accordance with these thoughts in order to keep your training in essential purity.

The patterns of the forms are of secondary importance. Of primary importance is expressing your potential, and to do this, you must use the basic elements of weight, speed, accuracy and concentration. It is impossible to destroy your target without weight. Likewise, it is impossible to destroy your target without speed, even though you may apply your weight. And, even though you may strike with speed and weight, you will be ineffective unless you watch your target and strike accurately. These are essential principles derived from natural philosophy which will help you to perform with good spirit.

The vital points of Taegeuk can only be maintained by making the indicated moves with precision and correct speed. You must maintain solid balance while executing these actions. If you do these things, you will come to understand the purpose and main thought behind Taegeuk. Begin your journey.

—Pu Gill Gwon

Publisher's Note: As a visual aid, chapters 2-12 each begin with a diagram. The explanations of the steps direct you to move along the lines and directions which are illustrated by these diagrams.

Contents

Chapter One
TECHNIQUES

This chapter introduces the basic techniques used in the Taegeuk forms. There are many more variations of these techniques possible, but these are the elements upon which the more advanced tae kwon do movements are based.

The primary contact areas of the body, both for defending, and for striking, are illustrated in the first section of the chapter. Section two covers the basic stances; section three, the methods of striking; and section four, the methods of defending.

When practicing these techniques, it is important to remember that in the forms, you will be required to coordinate the execution of these techniques with the movement of your feet. Stepping into stances, for example, will be accompanied by the simultaneous execution of blocks or strikes.

CONTACT
AREAS

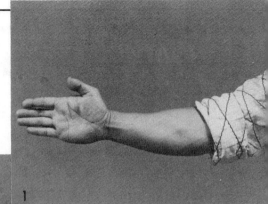

1

2

FIST
(Joomeok)

To form a fist, (1) extend your fingers out so that they are side by side, and your thumb is pointed outward from your palm at a right angle. Then (2) fold your fingers down so that the tips touch your palm, and your fingers are now pointing in toward your body. (3) Next, press the fingertips firmly into your palm by flexing them at the knuckles, and (4) fold your thumb over the closed fingers to secure the structure of the fist. Your fist must be tight at all times to prevent injury to yourself, and to insure the effectiveness of your blow.

3

4

Palm Side

WRIST
(Palmok)

The wrist is used primarily for blocking and deflecting blows. There are four sides to the wrist, and all four of these sides are utilized. In all cases, the area of contact is the part of the forearm just below the wrist.

Thumb Side

Ulna Side

Back Side

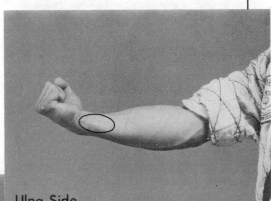

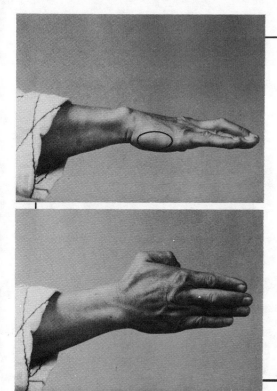

KNIFE HAND
(Sonnal)

In a knife hand, all the fingers are extended straight except the middle finger which is flexed slightly so that its tip is even with that of the index finger, and the tip of the thumb is pointed in toward the palm. The striking area is the edge of the hand just below the little finger.

RIDGE HAND
(Sonnal-Deung)

The reverse knife hand is the same as the knife hand except that the thumb is folded across the palm. The striking area is the edge of the hand just below the knuckle of the index finger.

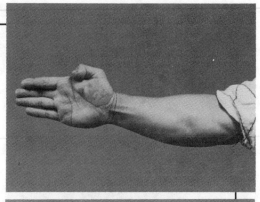

SPEAR HAND
(Pyonson-Keut)

The striking area of the spear hand is the tips of all the fingers except for the thumb and little finger, and it is important for the fingers to be pressed tightly together to support each other, and for the middle finger to be flexed slightly so that the striking tips of all the fingers make contact simultaneously.

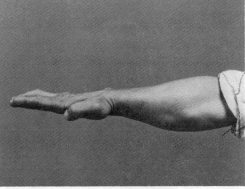

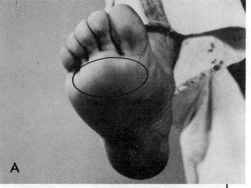

FOOT
(Bal)

When the foot is employed for kicking, two main areas are used: (A) The ball of the foot (apchook) which is the fleshy portion of the sole just below the toes—the toes, in this case, being curled back out of the way to protect them, and to expose the striking area; and (B) the outer edge of the foot (balnal) directly below the ankle.

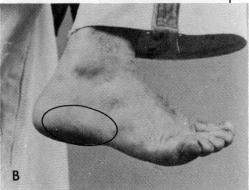

BACK FIST
(Deung-Joomeok)

A back fist is formed in the same way as a normal fist, but the striking area is the back of your knuckles rather than the front.

HAMMER FIST
(Me-Joomeok)

The structure of the hammer fist is also identical to the normal fist, but the striking area used in this case is the fleshy portion of your fist's edge just below the little finger.

ELBOW
(Palkoop)

The elbow is employed to strike by bending the arm in toward the body, and using the point of the elbow as the striking area. In the Taegeuk forms, an elbow strike is often accompanied by a pressing of the opposite palm on the striking area of the elbow to indicate contact.

KNEE
(Mooreup)

A strike using the knee is delivered properly by flexing the knee, and using the point of the kneecap as the striking area.

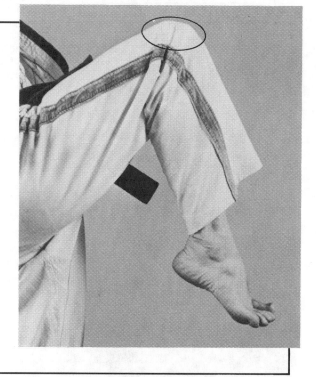

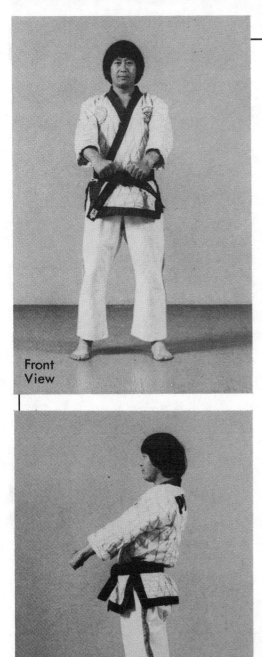

Front View

Side View

STANCES

READY STANCE
(Pyeonhi-Seogi)

In this stance, the feet are about shoulder-width apart, and are angled slightly outward. The accompanying arm position used throughout the Taegeuk series of forms is that in which the fists are held out in front of the lower abdomen about the width of one fist away from the body (*gibon-joonbi*).

BACK STANCE
(Dwitkoobi)

In the back stance, the lead foot is pointed forward. The back foot is pointed out at a right angle in relation to the lead foot. The feet are one normal walking step apart. The knee of the back leg is flexed, and as a result, the knee of the forward leg is also slightly flexed. The whole weight of the body rests on the back leg.

Front View

Side View

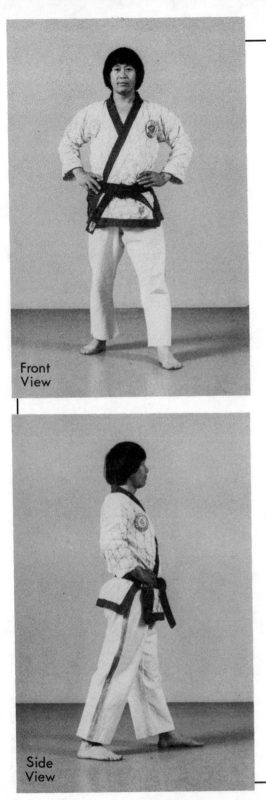

Front
View

Side
View

FORWARD STANCE
(Apseogi)

To assume the forward stance, take a normal walking step forward. At the point where both feet are on the ground, stop. That is the proper distance for the separation of your feet. Both knees should be straight but not locked. Your lead foot is pointed directly forward, and your rear foot should be pointed outward slightly. About 70 percent of your weight is on your lead foot.

EXTENDED FORWARD STANCE
(Apkoobi)

To assume the extended forward stance, use your normal walking step as a reference, and extend your lead foot forward one-and-a-half times the distance of that step. Bend the knee of that lead leg so that it comes directly over the lead foot. The angles of our feet are the same as for the forward stance.

Front View

Side View

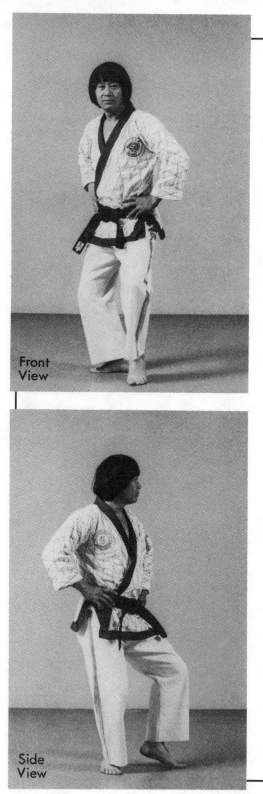

Front
View

Side
View

TIGER STANCE
(Beom-Seogi)

In the tiger stance, all of your weight should be on your back leg, and the knee of that leg is bent, and the back foot is pointed out slightly. Your forward leg should be one step forward, and the knee also bent, with the heel of the forward foot raised up so that only the ball of that foot makes contact with the floor.

CRANE STANCE
(Haktari-Seogi)

In the crane stance, one foot is raised off the floor, so that it rests against the inside of the knee of the supporting leg. The knee of the supporting leg is bent slightly.

Front View

Side View

27

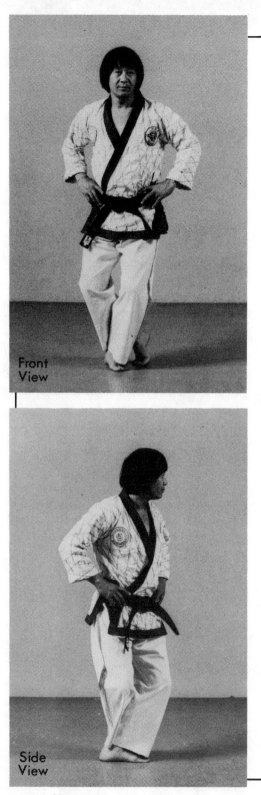

Front
View

Side
View

CROSS LEGGED STANCE
(Koa-Seogi)

In the cross legged stance, one leg is crossed in front of the other, and the body weight is evenly distributed on both feet.

STRIKING

Front View

Side View

FRONT PUNCH
(Bandae-Jireugi)

The front punch is executed with the fist of the same side as the lead foot. From the waist, with the palm side up, the fist is rotated as the arm is extended so that at full extension, the palm side of the fist is facing down.

Application: Here, the front punch is used to strike the chest of the opponent. The front punch can be used to attack any area in a sparring situation, but in the Taegeuk forms, it is used primarily for striking to the middle or the head.

APPLICATION

29

Front
View

Side
View

REVERSE FRONT PUNCH
(Baro-Jireugi)

The reverse front punch is executed in the same way as the front punch except with the fist of the opposite side of the lead foot.

Application: The reverse front punch technique is used here to strike to the middle of the opponent. Both the front punch and the reverse front punch may be executed from either a forward stance, or an extended forward stance.

APPLICATION

SPEAR THRUST
(Pyonson-Keut-Sewochireugi)

The spear thrust is executed by extending the spear hand forcefully with the thumb side of the hand facing upwards. The spear thrust is accompanied by a motion bringing the other open hand to a palm down position under the elbow of the striking arm in preparation for a block.

Application: This spear thrust to the opponent's middle is accompanied, as it is in the forms, by a simultaneous block by the other hand, countering the opponent's attack.

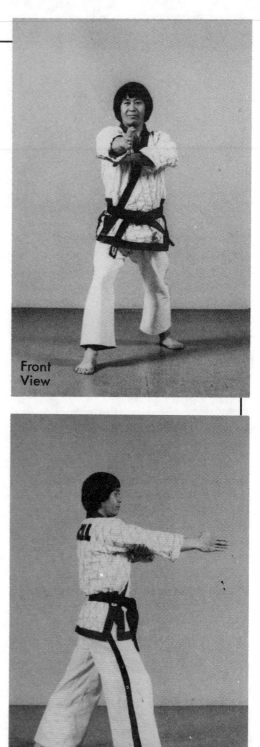

Front View

APPLICATION

Side View

31

Front
View

Side
View

ELBOW STRIKE
(Palkoop-Chagi)

This strike is executed by twisting the upper body, and swinging the elbow of the flexed arm forward to the target. *Application:* The elbow is employed here to attack the face of the opponent. Use of this technique is usually limited to close combat situations.

APPLICATION

1

FRONT KICK
(Apchagi)

The front kick is executed by (1) bringing the knee up, and (2) snapping the leg forward, using the ball of the foot as the striking surface
Application: The front kick can be used to attack almost any part of your opponent's body. Here, it is shown being used to strike the chin of the opponent.

2

APPLICATION

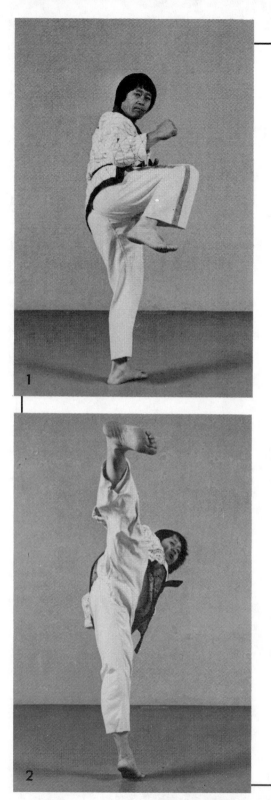

SIDE KICK
(Yeop-Chagi)

The side kick is executed by (1) raising the knee up, and snapping the leg out to the side, using the outer edge of the foot .as the striking surface.

Application: Speed in delivering the side kick depends very much upon flexibility in the hips and inner thighs. The side kick is shown here being applied to strike to the opponent's midsection.

APPLICATION

ROUND KICK
(Dollyo-Chagi)

The round kick is executed by (1) raising the knee up and rotating the hips in the direction of your target, then (2) snapping the leg out and around in an arc, using the ball of the foot as the striking surface.

Application: In addition to the power of snapping the leg out, the round kick also derives much of its effectiveness from the whipping motion of rotating the hips. It is shown here as a means of attacking the head.

1

2

APPLICATION

35

DEFENDING

1

LOW BLOCK
(Arae-Makki)

(1) Prepare by crossing your fists. (2) Pull the defending arm of the same side as your forward leg across your body, then (3) extend the defending arm downward to perform the block with the ulna side of the wrist. The *reverse low block (arae-an-makki)* is done the same way but with the arm opposite the forward leg.
Application: Defend against a low kick.

2

APPLICATION

3

INWARD MIDDLE BLOCK
(Momtong-Makki)

(1) Cock the defending arm, then (2) bring the arm forward forcefully, (3) rotating the wrist to perform the block with the ulna side of the wrist.
Application: Defend against a front punch.

2

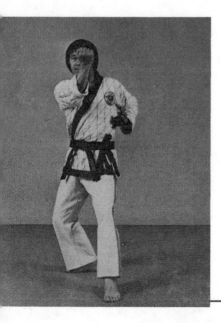

APPLICATION

OUTWARD MIDDLE BLOCK
(Momtong-Bakkat-Makki)

(1) Bring the defending arm to the opposite shoulder to cross with the other arm, then (2) spread both arms apart, and (3) execute the block outward with the ulna side of the wrist.
Application: Use to counter a front punch.

APPLICATION

HIGH BLOCK
(Eolgool-Makki)

(1) Cross both fists in front of your chest, then (2) spread both arms apart in opposite directions, and (3) perform the block upward with the ulna side of the wrist above the forehead.

Application: Counter a front punch attack to the head.

APPLICATION

1

DOUBLE BLOCK
(Hechyo-Makki)

(1) Begin by crossing your wrists over your chest. Then (2) bring them apart, rotating the wrists at the same time, and (3) perform the blocks outward with the ulna sides of the wrists.

Application: The double block is used here to counter a two handed grab by the opponent.

2

APPLICATION

3

CROSS BLOCK
(Eotgeoreo-Makki)
(1) Begin with both wrists in ready position at your sides. Then (2) bring both fists forward, rotating them at the same time, and (3) perform the block by crossing both wrists in front of your lower body, using the ulna sides as the contact area.

Application: The cross block is often used to defend against low kicks.

APPLICATION

Chapter Two

KEON

The first Taegeuk form is composed to accommodate white belts, and it is characterized by two kicking actions, one in the 14th, and one in the 16th steps. It includes the ready stance, the elemental walking movement, and both the forward and extended forward stances.

Being the first form, its actions are associated with the first concept of the *Book of Changes* which is called *keon*. Keon is the creative force which inhabits all physical forms. Keon is powerful and aggressive, and it is represented by heaven and light.

As a student, you are urged to consider this concept as you do this first form, and to allow it to influence the styling of your movements. The effect of these thoughts on your performance may be extremely subtle, but to the eyes of an expert, it is quite noticeable, and indeed, traditionally correct.

TAEGEUK ONE JANG
AT A GLANCE

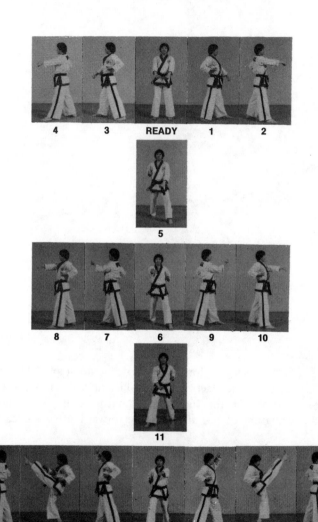

4 3 READY 1 2

5

8 7 6 9 10

11

16B 16A 15 12 13 14A 14B

END

18

17

LINE AND DIRECTION
OF MOVEMENT

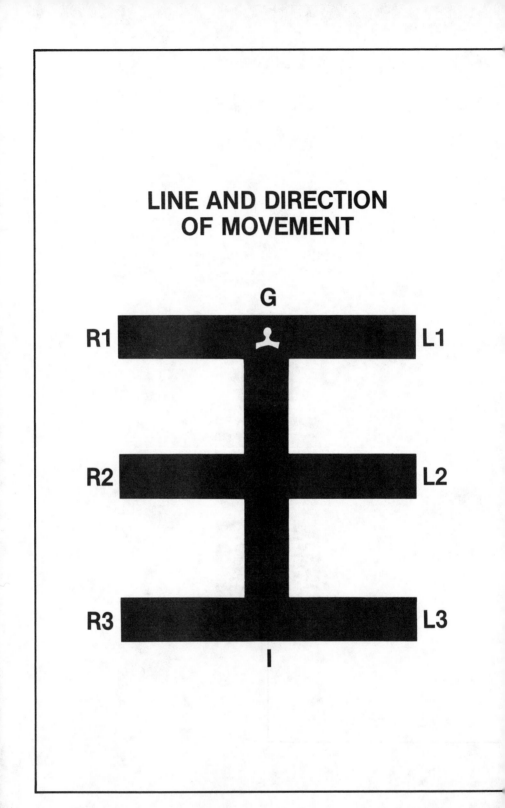

Ready
Stance

TAEGEUK ONE JANG

From the *ready stance*, (1) turn to the left, and place your left foot along the line L1, assuming a *left forward stance*, then simultaneously execute a

1

Continued

left low block. (2) Step forward into a *right forward stance* on line L1, and execute a *right front punch* to the middle. (3) Turn in a clockwise direction by pivoting on the ball of your left foot, placing your right foot on line R1, assuming a *right forward stance,* and execute a *right low block.* (4) Step forward into a *left forward stance* on line R1, and execute a *left front punch* to the middle. (5) Turn in a counterclockwise direction by pivoting on the ball of your right foot, and place your left foot toward I in a *left forward stance,* and simultaneously execute a *left low block,* (6) Then immediately execute a *right reverse front punch* to the middle from the same stance. (7) Turn in a clockwise direction by pivoting on the ball of your left foot, placing your right foot on line R2 in a *right forward stance,* and simultaneously execute a

3

4

6

7

Continued

left reverse inward middle block. (8) Move your left foot forward on line R2, assuming a *left forward stance,* and execute a *right reverse front punch* to the middle. (9) Pivot on the ball of your right foot, turning in a counterclockwise direction, and move your left foot to line L2 into a *left forward stance,* and execute a *right reverse inward middle block.* (10) Step forward with your right foot on line L2 into a *right forward stance,* and execute a *left reverse front punch* to the middle. (11) Pivot on the ball of your left foot, turning clockwise, and step forward with your right foot toward I into a *right forward stance,* and execute a *right low block,* (12) Then immediately execute a *left reverse front punch* to the middle from the same stance. (13) Pivot counterclockwise on the ball of your right foot, and step forward with your left into a *left forward stance* on line L3, and simultaneously execute a *left high block.* (14A) Execute a *right front*

9

10

3

14A

kick, and (14B) drop your right foot forward on line L3, assuming a *right forward stance,* and execute a *right front punch* to the middle. (15) Pivot clockwise on the ball of your left foot, and move your right foot to line R3, assuming a *right forward stance,* and execute a *right high block.* (16A) Execute a *left front kick,* and (16B) drop your left foot forward on line R3, assuming a *left forward stance,* and execute a *left front punch* to the middle. (17) Pivot on the ball of your right foot, turning clockwise, and placing your left foot forward toward G, assuming a *left forward stance,* and execute a *left low block.* (18) Step forward with your right toward G, assuming a *right forward stance,* and execute a *right front punch* to the middle, and yell. (19) Pivot on the ball of your right foot, turning counterclockwise to face in the direction of I, and bring your left foot adjacent to your right foot, assuming the *ready stance.*

14B

16B

FRONT VIEW

17

15

16A

FRONT
VIEW

18

19

End

Chapter Three

TAE

T he second form in the Taegeuk series is composed for the training of students of yellow belt rank. In addition to the actions presented in the previous chapter, this form introduces the front punch that is directed toward the head of the imagined adversary as a new technique.

Philosophically, this form correlates to the concept of *tae* which means joy. Tae is of a spiritually uplifting nature, but is not aggressive. It is serene and gentle instead.

In compliance with these characteristics then, the actions of this form should be performed with ease and fluidity; without the sense of struggling against your limitations, but nevertheless, living fully within them. Tae is symbolized by the image of a lake.

TAEGEUK TWO JANG
AT A GLANCE

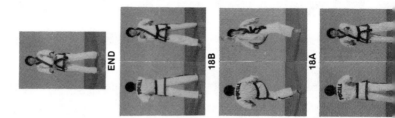

END

18B

18A

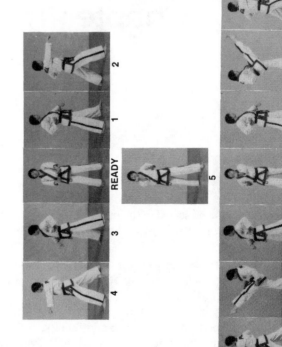

READY

1

2

3

4

5

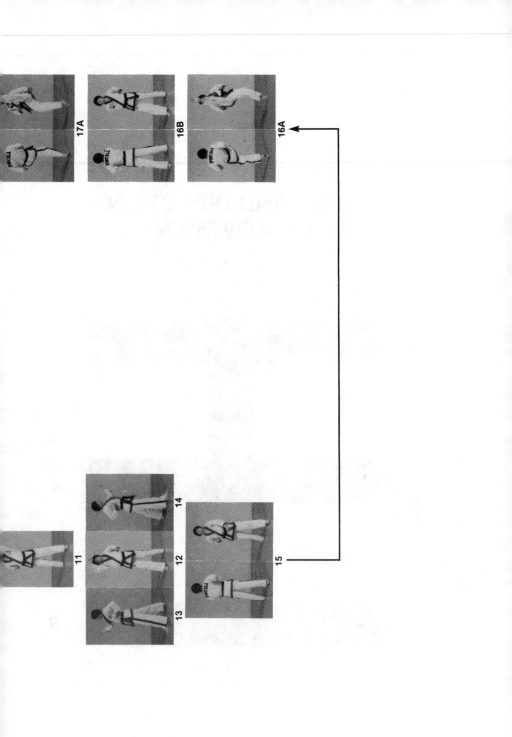

LINE AND DIRECTION
OF MOVEMENT

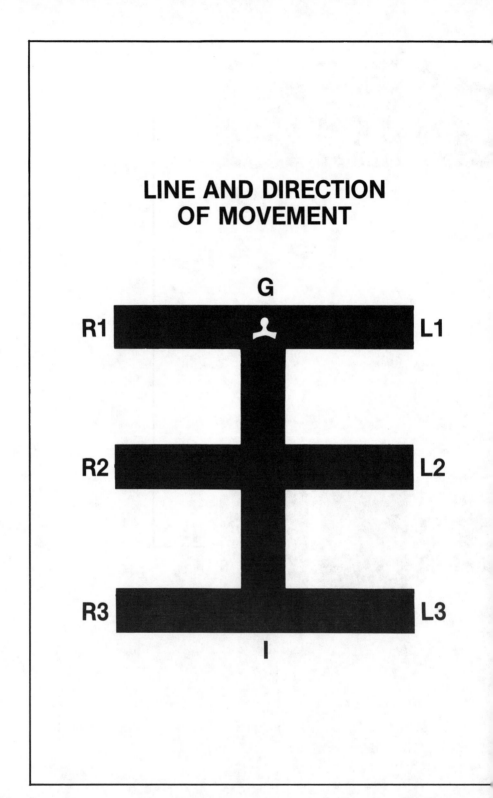

Ready Stance

TAEGEUK TWO JANG

From the *ready stance*, (1) turn counterclockwise to the left, and place your left foot forward on line L1, assuming a *left forward stance*, and

1

Continued

execute a *left low block*. (2) Step forward with your right foot on line L1 into a *right extended forward stance*, and execute a *right front punch* to the middle. (3) Pivot clockwise on the ball of your left foot, and place your right foot on line R1, assuming a *right forward stance*, and execute a *right low block*. (4) Step forward with your left foot on line R1 into a *left extended forward stance*, and execute a *left front punch* to the middle. (5) Pivot counterclockwise on the ball of your right foot, and place your left foot one step forward toward I, assuming a *left forward stance*, and execute a *right reverse inward middle block*. (6) Step forward with your right foot toward I, assuming a *right forward stance*, and execute a *left reverse inward middle*

3

5

6

61

Continued

block. (7) Pivot counterclockwise on the ball of your right foot, placing your left foot forward on line L2 into a *left forward stance*, and execute a *left low block.* (8A) Execute a *right front kick*, and (8B) drop right foot forward on line L2, assuming a *right extended forward stance*, and execute a *right front punch* to the head. (9) Pivot clockwise on the ball of your left foot, bringing your right one step forward on line R2, assuming a *right forward stance*, and execute a *right low block.* (10A) Execute a *left front kick*, and (10B) drop your left foot forward on line R2, and execute a *left front punch*

7

9

8A

8B

10A

10B

Continued

to the head. (11) Pivot counterclock-wise on the ball of your right foot, and place your left foot forward toward I, assuming a *left forward stance*, and execute a *left high block*. (12) Step forward with your right foot toward I, assuming a *right forward stance*, and execute a *right high block*. (13) Pivot counterclockwise on the ball of your right foot, bringing your left foot forward on line R3, assuming a *left forward stance*, and execute a *right inward middle block*. (14) Pivot counterclockwise on the ball of your left foot, placing your right foot forward on line L3, assuming a *right forward stance*, and execute a *left inward middle block*. (15) Pivot counterclockwise on the ball of your right foot, placing your left foot forward toward G, assuming a *left forward stance*. (16A) Execute a

12

13

FRONT
VIEW

15

16A

FRONT
VIEW

Continued

16B

right front kick, and (16B) drop your right foot forward toward G, assuming a *right forward stance*, and execute a *right front punch* to the middle. (17A) Execute a *left front kick*, and (17B) drop your left foot forward toward G, assuming a *left forward stance*, and execute a *left front punch* to the middle. (18A) Execute a *right front kick*, and (18B) drop your right foot forward toward G, assuming a *right forward stance*, and execute a *right front punch* to the middle, and yell. (19) Pivot counterclockwise on the ball of your right foot, to face in the direction of I, and bring your left foot adjacent to your right, assuming the *ready stance*.

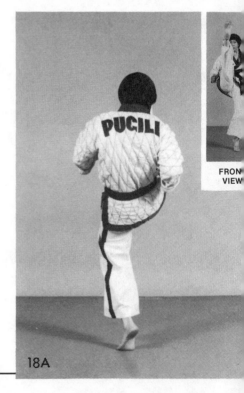

18A

FRONT
VIEW

17A

FRONT
VIEW

17B

FRONT
VIEW

8B

19

End

Chapter Four

RI

s with the previous form, proficiency in performing Taegeuk three jang is required of students of yellow belt rank and higher. The moves incorporated here, however, are more varied, and demand variety in quickness and strength on the part of the person performing as well.

Ri is the philosophical correlative of this form; and ri means fire and the sun. So, the movements of this form must emulate the qualities of fire—that of a flickering energy, of unpredictable pace and styling, and of quiet followed by great excitement or great passion—but continually moving, burning.

In this form, many moves are combined in quick succession, such as front kicks followed instantly by double front punches. This form also introduces the outward middle block with a knife hand and the knife hand strike as new techniques.

END | 20C | 20B | 20A

TAEGEUK THREE JANG AT A GLANCE

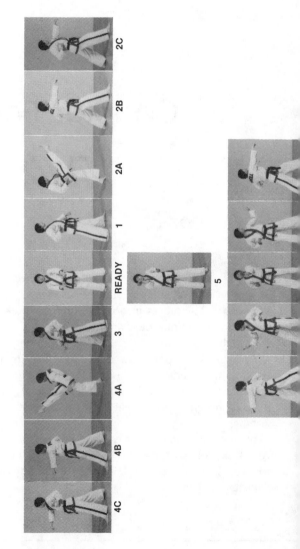

READY | 1 | 2A | 2B | 2C

3 | 4A | 4B | 4C

5

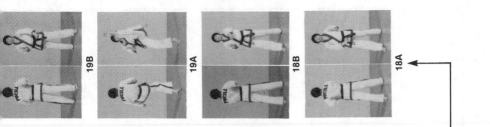

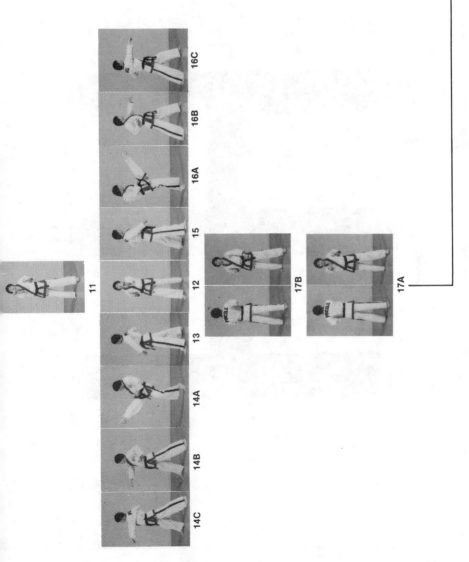

LINE AND DIRECTION
OF MOVEMENT

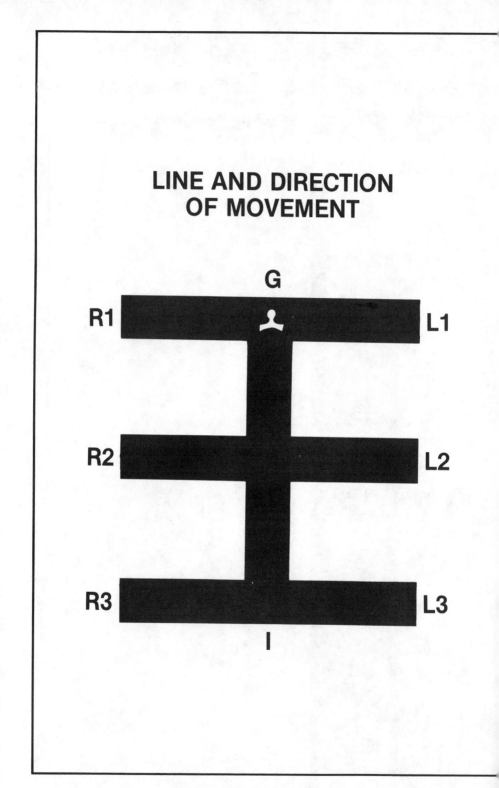

Ready
Stance

TAEGEUK THREE JANG

From the *ready stance*, (1) turn to the left, placing your left foot on line L1, assuming a *left forward stance*, and

1

73 Continued

2A

executing a *left low block*. (2A) Execute a *right front kick*, and (2B) drop your right foot forward on line L1, assuming a *right extended forward stance*, and execute a *right front punch* to the middle, then (2C) immediately follow with a *left reverse front punch* to the middle from the same stance. (3) Pivot clockwise on the ball of your left foot, stepping forward with your right foot on line R1, assuming a *right forward stance*, and execute a *right low block*. (4A) Execute a *left front kick*, and (4B) drop your left foot forward on line R1, assuming a *left extended forward stance*, and execute a *left front punch* to the middle,

3

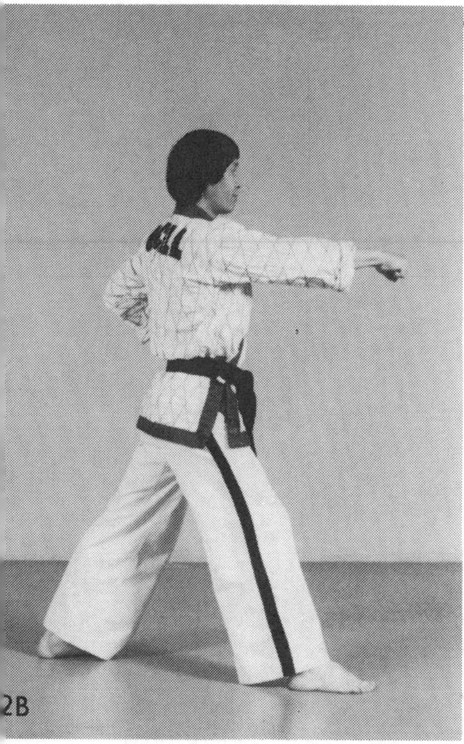
2B

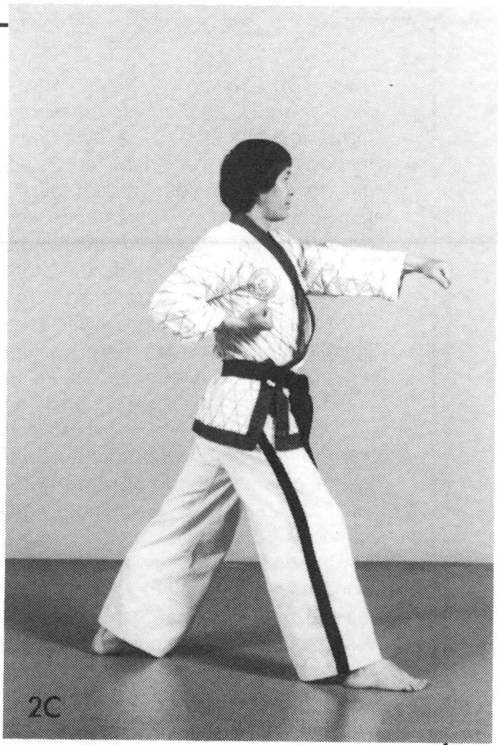
2C

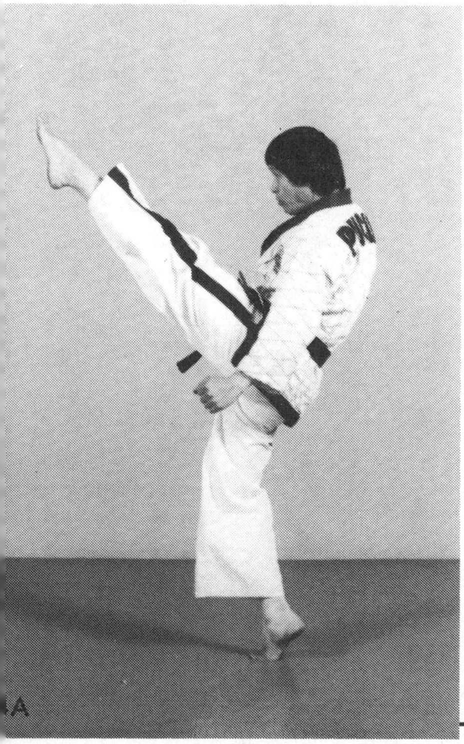
4A

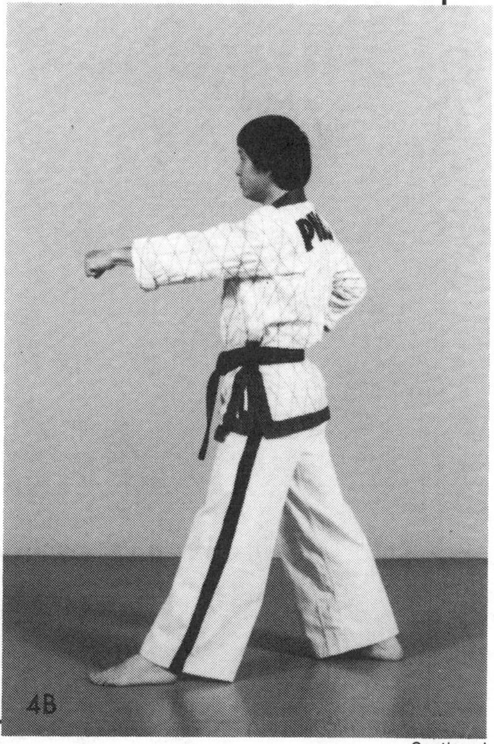
4B

Continued

then (4C) immediately follow with a *right reverse front punch* to the middle from the same stance. (5) Pivot counterclockwise on your right foot, stepping forward with your left foot toward I, assuming a *left forward stance*, and execute a *right knife hand strike* to the neck. (6) Step forward with your right foot toward I, assuming a *right forward stance*, and execute a *left knife hand strike* to the neck. (7) Turn to the left, and bring your left foot forward on line L2, assuming a *back stance* on your right leg, and execute a *left outward middle block* with a knife hand. (8) Immediately step forward with your left foot on line L2, assuming a *right extended forward stance,* and execute a *right reverse front punch.* (9) Pivot clockwise on the ball of your left foot, moving your right foot one step forward on line R2, assuming a *back stance* on your left leg, and execute an *outward middle block* with the knife hand. (10) Then, immediately step for-

4C

7

8

5

6

9

10

ward with your right foot on line R2, assuming a *right extended forward stance,* and execute a *left reverse punch* to the middle. (11) Pivot counterclockwise on the ball of your right foot, and place your left foot one step forward toward I, assuming a *left forward stance,* and execute a *right inward middle block.* (12) Step forward with your right foot toward I, assuming a *right forward stance,* and execute a *left reverse inward middle block.* (13) Pivot counterclockwise on the ball of your right foot, moving your left foot forward on line R3, assuming a *left forward stance,* and execute a *left low block.* (14A) Execute a *right front kick,* and (14B) drop your right foot forward on line R3, assuming a *right extended forward stance,* and execute a *right front punch* to the middle, (14C) followed instantly by a *left reverse front punch* to the middle from the same stance. (15) Pivot counter-

11

14A

14B

12

13

14C

15

Continued

clockwise on the ball of your left foot, moving your right foot forward on line L3, assuming a *right front stance,* and execute a *right low block.* (16A) Execute a *left front kick,* and (16B) drop your left foot forward on line L3, assuming a *left extended forward stance,* and execute a *left front punch* to the middle, (16C) followed instantly by a *right reverse front punch* to the middle from the same stance. (17A) Pivot counterclockwise on the ball of your right foot, moving your left foot forward toward G, assuming a *left forward stance,* and execute a *left low block,* (17B) then, immediately execute a *right reverse front punch* to the middle from the same stance. (18A) Step forward with your right foot toward G, assuming a *right forward stance,* and execute a *right low block,* (18B) then, immediately execute a *left reverse front punch* to the middle from the

16A

FRONT VIEW

FRONT VIEW

17A

17B

16B

16C

FRONT
VIEW

FRONT
VIEW

18A

18B

Continued

same stance. (19A) Execute a *left front kick,* and (19B) drop your left foot forward toward G, assuming a *left forward stance,* and execute a *left low block,* (19C) followed instantly by a *right reverse front punch* to the middle from the same stance. (20A) Execute a *right front kick,* and (20B) drop your right foot forward towards G, assuming a *right forward stance,* and execute a *right low block,* (20C) followed immediately by a *left reverse front punch* to the middle from the same stance, and yell. (21) Pivot counterclockwise on the ball of your right foot to face in the direction of I, and bring your left foot adjacent to your right, assuming the *ready stance.*

FRONT
VIEW

19A

FRONT
VIEW

FRONT
VIEW

20A

20B

FRONT
VIEW

9B

FRONT
VIEW

19C

FRONT
VIEW

20C

21

End

Chapter Five

JIN

Taegeuk four jang applies the principles of *jin,* which stands for thunder—the element of fear and trembling which occasionally enters our lives.

Because tae kwon do is comprised exclusively of virtuous actions, Taegeuk expresses fear and trembling in the only way that virtue can—stoically, as a passing thunderstorm which nourishes the soul. Virtue, therefore, defines fear as courage.

This form, as a consequence, contains many postures that display composure and strong balance such as blocks in combination with strikes and, front kicks that require the performer to kick with force but immediately recover into back stances. Students of the green belt rank and higher are required to master this form.

TAEGEUK FOUR JANG AT A GLANCE

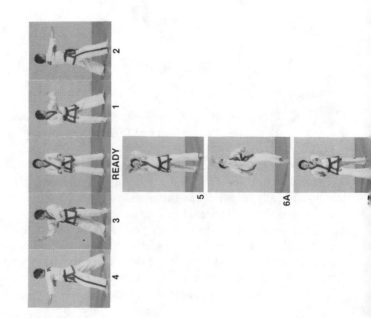

READY 1 2 3 4

5 6A

20A 20B 20C END

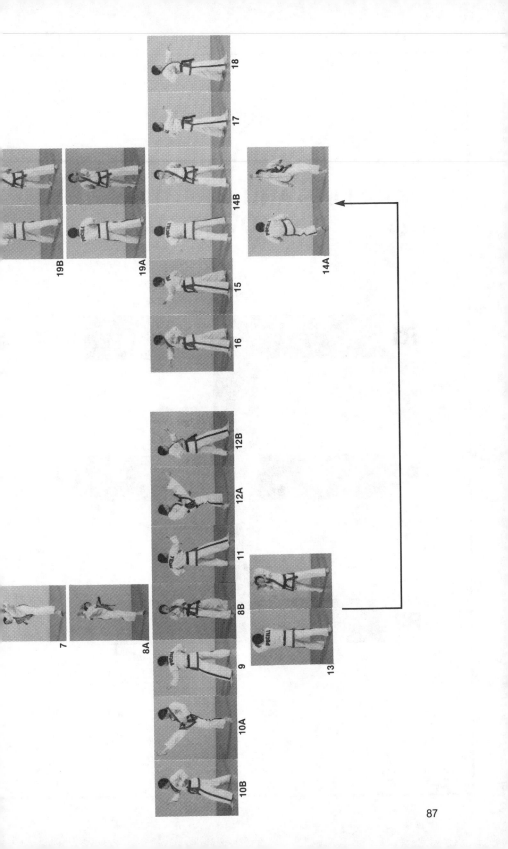

19B

19A

18

17

14B

15

16

14A

12B

12A

11

8B

9

10A

10B

7

8A

13

87

LINE AND DIRECTION
OF MOVEMENT

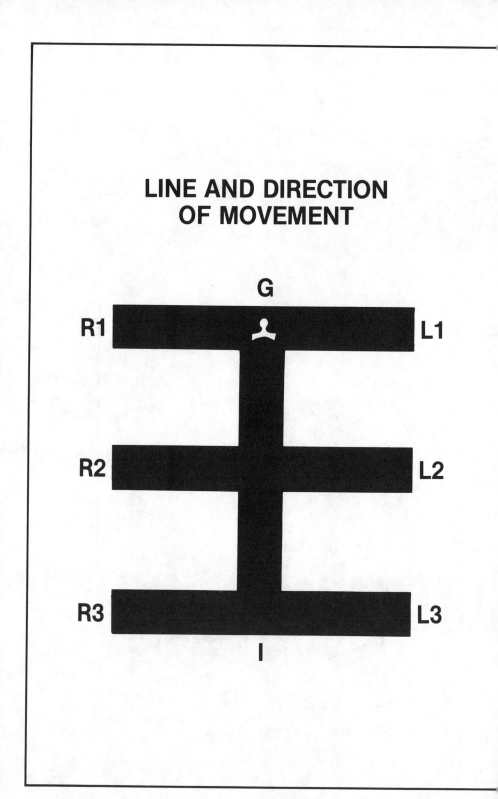

Ready Stance

TAEGEUK FOUR JANG

From the *ready stance,* (1) turn to your left, stepping forward with your left foot on line L1, assuming a *back stance* on your right leg, and execute a *left outward middle block* with the

1

Continued

knife hand. (2) Step forward with your right foot on line L1, assuming a *right extended forward stance*, and execute a *right spear thrust* to the middle, bringing your open left hand palm down below the elbow of your extended right arm. (3) Pivot clockwise on the ball of your left foot, moving your right foot forward on line R1, assuming a *back stance* on your left leg, and execute a *right outward middle block* with the knife hand. (4) Step forward with your left foot on line R1, assuming a *left extended forward stance*, and execute a *left spear thrust* to the middle, bringing your open right hand palm down below the elbow of your extended left arm. (5) Pivot counterclockwise on the ball of your right foot, moving your left foot forward toward I, assuming a *left extended forward stance*, and execute a *left high block* with the knife hand, and simultaneously, *a right knife hand strike* to the neck, maintaining both hands in their blocking and striking positions respectively, (6A) execute a *right front kick*, and then,

2

4

3

5

6A

91

Continued

6B

(6B) drop your right foot forward toward I, assuming a *right extended forward stance*, and execute a *left reverse front punch* to the middle. (7) Execute a *left side kick*, and drop your left foot forward toward I, assuming a *left extended forward stance*, then immediately (8A) execute a *right side kick,* and (8B) drop your right foot forward toward I, assuming a *back stance* on your left leg, and execute a *right outward middle block* with the knife hand. (9) Pivot counterclockwise on the ball of your right foot, moving your left foot forward on line R3, assuming a *back stance* on your right leg, and execute a *left outward middle block* with the ulna side of the wrist. (10A) Execute

8B

7

8A

9

10A

Continued

10B

a *right front kick,* and (10B) drop your right foot backward to its original position assuming a *back stance* on your right leg, and execute a *right inward middle block* with the ulna side of the wrist. (11) Keeping both feet in the same place, turn clockwise to face the direction of L3, assuming a *back stance* on your left leg, and execute a *right outward middle block* with the ulna side of the wrist. (12A) Execute a *left front kick,* and (12B) drop your left foot backward to its original position, assuming a *back stance* on your left leg, and execute a *left inward middle block* with the ulna side of the wrist. (13) Keeping your right foot in the same position, turn in the direction of G, moving your left foot forward toward G, assuming a *left extended forward stance,* and execute a *left high block* with the knife hand, and simultaneously, a *right knife hand strike* to the neck, (14A)

12B

1

12A

FRONT
VIEW

13

14A

FRONT
VIEW

95

Continued

FRONT
VIEW

Execute a *right front kick*, and (14B) drop your right foot forward toward G, assuming a *right extended forward stance,* and execute a *right back fist punch* to the face. (15) Keeping both feet in the same place, turn counterclockwise to face in the direction of R2, assuming a *left forward stance*, and execute a *left inward middle block*. (16) Execute a *right reverse front punch* to the middle from the same stance. (17) Keeping both feet in the same place, turn clockwise to face in the direction of L2, and execute a *right outward middle block*. (18) Execute a *left reverse front punch* to the middle from the same stance. (19A) Keeping your right foot in the same place, turn counterclockwise to face in the direction of G, moving your left foot forward toward G, assuming a *left forward stance,* and execute a *left inward middle block,*

14B

17

5

16

FRONT
VIEW

8

19A

Continued

then (19B) execute a *right reverse front punch* to the middle from the same stance, and instantly (19C) execute a *left front punch* to the middle from the same stance. (20A) Step forward with your right foot toward G, assuming a *right extended forward stance,* and execute a *right inward middle block,* then quickly (20B) execute a *left reverse front punch* to the middle from the same stance, and immediately (20C) execute a *right front punch* to the middle from the same stance, and yell. (21) Turn counterclockwise to face in the direction of I, and move your right foot adjacent to your left, assuming the *ready stance.*

19B

FRONT VIEW

20B

FRONT VIEW

9C

FRONT
VIEW

20A

FRONT
VIEW

20C

FRONT
VIEW

21

End

Chapter Six

SEON

This group of Taegeuk actions expresses a concept called *seon,* the fifth of the eight concepts in the great circle of the *Jooyeok,* the *Book of Changes.* Seon encompasses the characteristics of wind: gentle and strong; yielding and penetrating; soothing and destructive; invisible, yet manifesting, in concrete terms, the interplay of the um and yang taking place beyond time. The concept of seon is of a subtle nature, but pure, without evil intent; it is a state of being, the state of being like the wind.

A sweeping hammer fist strike, and a leap forward into the cross legged stance are introduced for the first time in the Taegeuk series of forms. The powerful elbow strike is also used, as are quick flowing combinations.

Students of the rank of blue belt are required to be proficient in this as well as the preceding forms.

TAEGEUK FIVE JANG AT A GLANCE

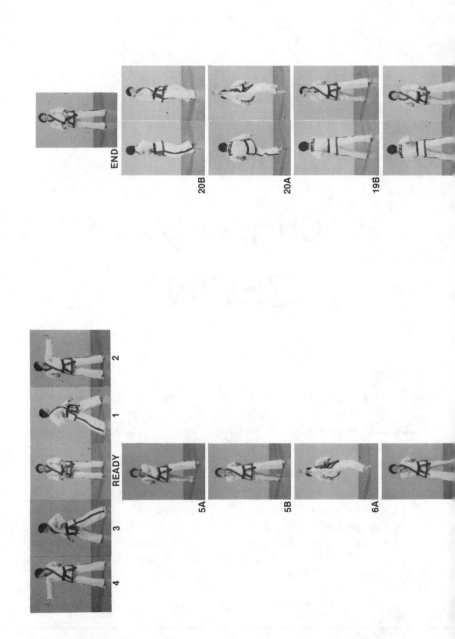

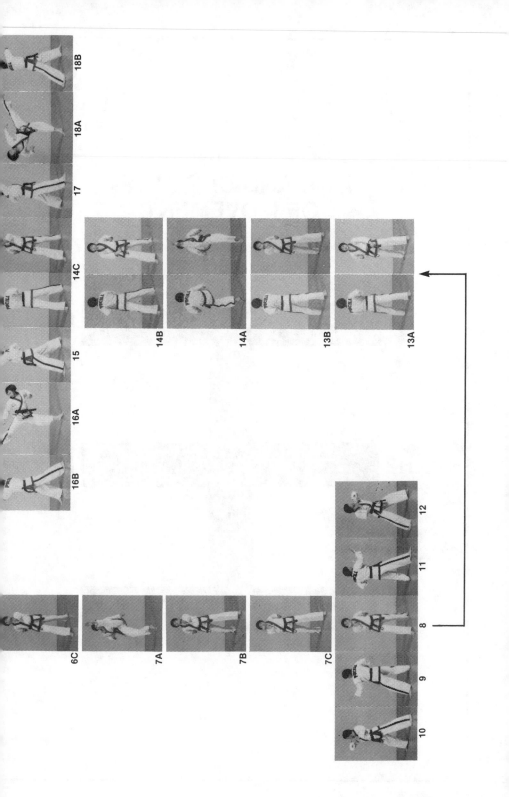

LINE AND DIRECTION OF MOVEMENT

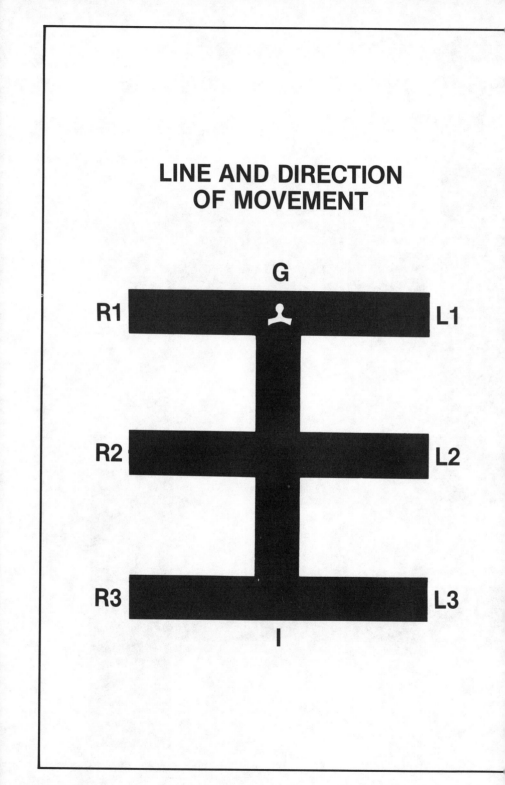

Ready Stance

TAEGEUK FIVE JANG

From the *ready stance*, (1) turn to the left, and step forward with your left foot on line L1, assuming a *left extended forward stance*, and execute a

1

105

left low block. (2) Bring your left foot back to its original *ready stance* position, and strike downward with a *left hammer fist*, by bringing your left arm over in an arc from the waist, rotating the wrist, and extending the arm out to the side at the same time. (3) Pivot clockwise on the ball of your left foot to face R1, and step forward with your right foot on line R1, assuming a *right extended forward stance,* and execute a *right low block.* (4) Bring your right foot back to its original *ready stance* position, and execute a downward strike with a *right hammer fist*, by bringing the right arm over in an arc from the waist, rotating the wrist and extending the arm out to the side at the same time. (5A) Step forward with your left foot toward I, assuming a *left extended forward stance,* and execute a *left inward middle block*, (5B) followed by a *right reverse inward middle block* from the same stance. (6A) Ex-

4

B

6A

107

Continued

6B

ecute a *right front kick,* and (6B) drop your right foot forward toward I, assuming a *right extended forward stance,* and execute a *right back fist strike* to the face, (6C) followed by a *left reverse inward middle block* from the same stance. (7A) Execute a *left front kick,* and (7B) drop your left foot forward toward I, assuming a *left extended forward stance,* and execute a *left back fist strike* to the face, (7C) followed by a *right reverse inward middle block* from the same stance. (8) Step forward with your right toward I, assuming a *right extended forward stance,* and execute a *right back fist*

7B

6C

7A

7C

8

Continued

strike to the face. (9) Pivot counterclockwise on the ball of your right foot, and step forward with your left foot on line R3, assuming a *backstance* on your right leg, and execute a *left outward middle block* with the knife hand. (10) Step with your right foot on line R3, assuming a *right extended forward stance*, and execute a *right elbow strike* to the middle, supporting your right fist with your left palm. (11) Pivot counterclockwise on the ball of your left leg, moving your right foot forward on line L3, assuming a *back stance* on your left leg, and executing a *right outward middle block* with the knife hand. (12) Step forward with your left foot on line L3, assuming a *left extended forward stance*, and execute a *left elbow strike* to the middle, supporting your left fist in your right palm. (13A) Pivot counterclockwise on the ball of your right foot, stepping forward with your left foot toward G, assuming a *left extended forward stance*, and execute a *left low block*. (13B) Then, execute a *right reverse inward middle block* from the same

0

11

FRONT
VIEW

FRONT
VIEW

13A

13B

Continued

stance. (14A) Execute a *right front kick,* and (14B) drop your right foot forward toward G, assuming a *right extended forward stance,* and execute a *right low block,* (14C) followed by a *left reverse middle block.* (15) Turn counterclockwise, keeping your right foot in the same place, and moving your left foot forward on line R2, assuming a *left extended forward stance,* and execute a *left high block.* (16A) Execute a right side kick, and (16B) drop your right foot forward on line R2, assuming a *right extended forward stance,* and execute a *right elbow strike* to the middle, using your left palm to indicate contact. (17) Pivot clockwise on the ball of your left foot, stepping forward with your right foot on line L2, assuming a *right extended forward stance,* and execute a *right*

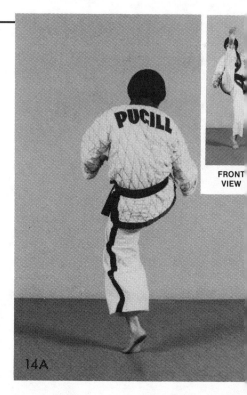

FRONT VIEW

14A

15

16A

FRONT VIEW

FRONT VIEW

14B

14C

16B

17

113

Continued

high block. (18A) Execute a *left side kick,* and (18B) drop your left foot forward on line L2, assuming a *left extended forward stance,* and execute a *right elbow strike,* using your left palm to indicate contact. (19A) Pivot counterclockwise on the ball of your right foot, stepping forward with your left foot toward G, assuming a *left extended forward stance,* and execute a *left low block,* then (19B) execute a *right reverse inward middle block* from the same stance. (20A) Execute a *right front kick,* and (20B) jump forward on your right foot toward G, and bring your left foot up behind your right, crossing your right foot, assuming a *cross legged stance,* and execute a *right back fist strike* to the face, and yell. (21) Pivot counterclockwise on the ball of your right foot, to face in the direction of I, assuming the *ready stance.*

18A

FRONT VIEW

FRONT VIEW

19B

20A

114

18B

19A

FRONT
VIEW

20B

SIDE
VIEW

21

End

Chapter Seven

GAM

he dramatic expressions of Taegeuk six jang are defined by the concept of *gam*—water: flowing, shapeless, always true to its nature, incorporating all obstacles in its path in its own sense of flow. It is important for the practitioner to recognize this as a type of confidence, of always knowing whatever difficulties or hardships he may encounter in life, or in the pracitice of his art, there exists no doubt of overcoming them as long as he retains the qualities of acceptance, flow, and natural integrity.

This set of movements must be performed with fluidity, and the feeling that every action is exactly what is called for to overcome the situation at each particular instant.

Students of the rank of blue belt are required to be proficient in this and the preceding forms.

TAEGEUK SIX JANG AT A GLANCE

4B 4A 3 READY 1 2A 2B

5

10B 10A 9B 9A 6 7A 7B 8A 8B

11

12

17B 17A 16 13 14 15A 15B

END

23

22

21

20

19

18

LINE AND DIRECTION OF MOVEMENT

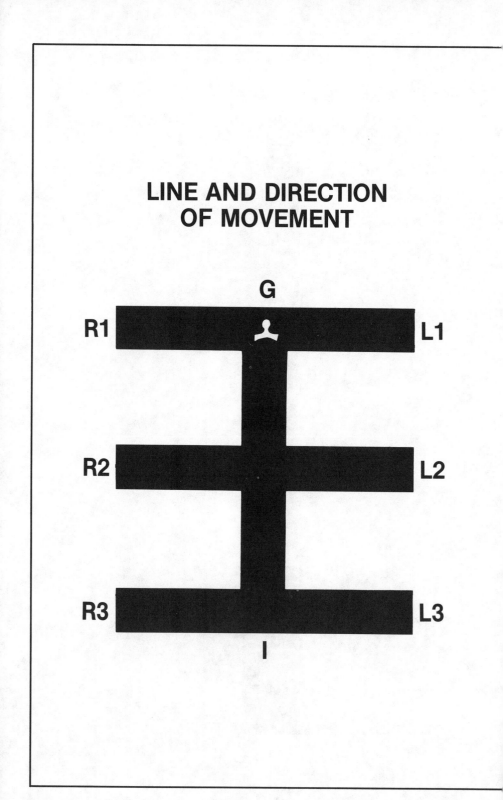

TAEGEUK SIX JANG

From the *ready stance*, (1) turn to the left, and step forward with your left foot on the line L1, assuming a *left extended forward stance,* and execute a

Ready Stance

1

Continued

2A

left low block. (2A) Execute a *right front kick,* and (2B) drop the right foot back to its original place, assuming a *back stance* on your right leg, and execute a *left outward middle block* with the ulna side of the wrist. (3) Pivot clockwise on the ball of your left foot, and step forward with your right on line R1, assuming a *right extended forward stance,* and execute a *right low block.* (4A) Execute a *left front kick,* and (4B) drop the left foot back to its original place, assuming a *back stance* on your left foot, and execute a *right outward middle block.* (5) Turn in the direction of I, and step forward with your left foot toward I, assuming a *left extended forward stance,* and execute a *right reverse outward mid-*

4A

2B

3

4B

5

Continued

6

dle block with the knife hand. (6) Execute a *right round kick.* (7A) Drop your right foot forward toward I, then turn counterclockwise, and step forward with your left on line L2, assuming a *left extended forward stance,* and execute a *left outward high block* with the ulna side of the wrist, (7B) then execute a *right reverse front punch* to the middle from the same stance. (8A) Execute a *right front kick,* and (8B) drop your right foot forward on line L2, assuming a *right extended forward stance,* and execute a *left reverse front punch* to the middle. (9A) Pivot clockwise on the ball of your left foot, and step forward with your right on line R2, and execute a *right outward high block* with the ulna side

8A

7A

7B

8B

9A

Continued

9B

of the wrist, (9B) then immediately execute a *left reverse front punch* to the middle. (10A) Execute a *left front kick,* and (10B) drop your left foot forward on line R2, assuming a *left extended forward stance,* and execute a *right reverse front punch* to the middle. (11) Pivot counterclockwise on the ball of your right foot to face in the direction of I, bringing your left foot adjacent to your right into the *ready stance,* and execute a *double low block* with the ulna sides of the wrists. (12) Step forward with your right foot towards I, assuming a *right extended forward stance,* and execute a *right reverse outward middle block* with the knife hand. (13) Execute a *left round kick,*

11

10A

10B

2

13

Continued

and yell. (14) Drop your left foot forward toward I, and pivot counterclockwise on the ball of your left foot, stepping forward with your right on line L3, and execute a *right low block.* (15A) Execute a *left front kick,* and (15B) drop your left foot back to its original place, assuming a *back stance* on your left leg, and execute a *right outward middle block* with the ulna side of the wrist. (16) Pivot clockwise on the ball of your right foot, stepping forward with your left foot on line R3, and execute a *left low block.* (17A) Execute a *right front kick,* and (17B) drop your right foot back to its original place, assuming a *back stance* on your right foot, and execute a *left outward middle block* with the ulna side of the

14

16

15A

15B

17A

17B

Continued

wrist. (18) Keeping the left foot in the same place, turn counterclockwise by moving your right foot around behind you, and face in the direction of I, assuming a *back stance* on your right leg, and execute a *left outward middle block* with the knife hand. (19) Step backward with your left foot, assuming a *back stance* on your left leg, and execute a *right outward middle block* with the knife hand. (20) Step backward with your right, assuming a *left extended forward stance,* and execute a *left inward middle block* with the heel of your palm, and (21) execute a *right reverse front punch* to the middle from the same stance. (22) Step backward with your left foot, assuming a *right extended forward stance,* and execute a *right inward middle block* with the heel of your palm, and (23) execute a *left reverse front punch* to the middle from the same stance. (24) Bring your right foot back to an adjacent position with your left, assuming the *ready stance.*

18

21

22

19

20

23

24

End

Chapter Eight

GAN

T he seventh series of Taegeuk actions applies a concept called *gan,* meaning "top stop," the seventh of the eight concepts of the *Jooyeok.* The Taegeuk forms interpret gan, symbolized by the image of a mountain, as the principle of stability. This stability is defined as the structural soundness which results from having resolved one's ambition to touch heaven into the limitations of excellent form. This resolution is of a noble and majestic character; thus, the image of the mountain.

The tiger stance, in which most of your weight is settled on the back leg expresses this peculiar stabililty which also contains ambition. These actions use the tiger stance repeatedly.

Students of the rank of red or brown belt are required to be proficient in this and the preceding forms.

TAEGEUK SEVEN JANG AT A GLANCE

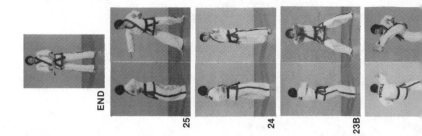

END 25 24 23B

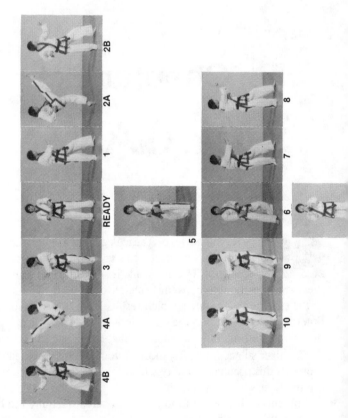

2B 2A 1 READY 3 4A 4B
8 7 6 5 9 10

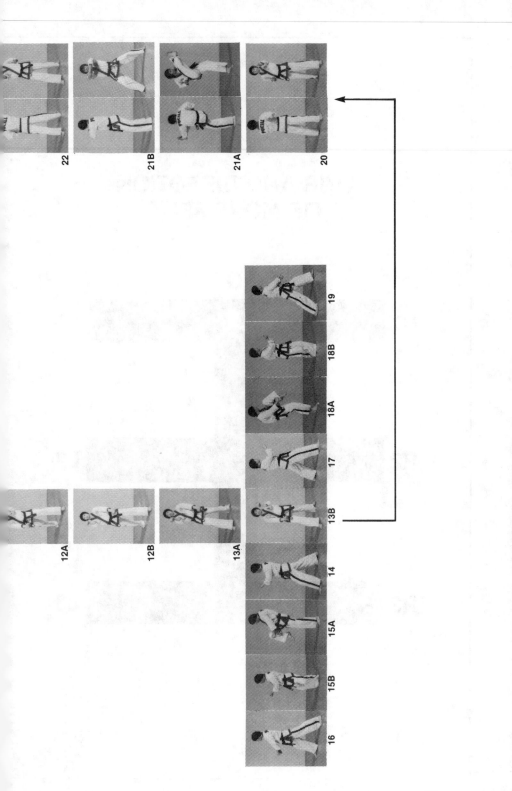

22

21B

21A

20

19

18B

18A

17

13B

14

15A

15B

16

12A

12B

13A

LINE AND DIRECTION
OF MOVEMENT

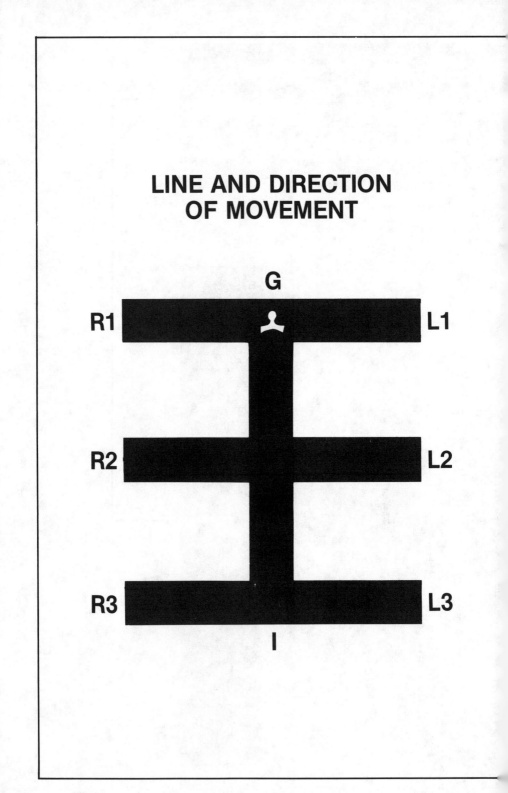

Ready Stance

TAEGEUK SEVEN JANG

From the *ready stance*, (1) turn your body counterclockwise to face L1, assuming a *tiger stance* on your right leg, and execute a *right inward middle*

1

Continued

2A

block with the heel of your palm. (2A) Execute a *right front kick,* and (2B) return the right foot to its original position, assuming a *tiger stance* on your right leg, and execute a *left inward middle block* with the ulna side of the wrist. (3) Pivot clockwise on the ball of your left foot to face R1, assuming a *tiger stance* on your left leg, and execute a *left inward middle block* with the heel of your palm. (4A) Execute a *left front kick*, and (4B) return the left foot to its original position, assuming a *tiger stance* on your left leg, and execute a *right inward middle block* with the ulna side of the wrist. (5) Turning counterclockwise, place your left foot forward in the direction of I, assuming a *back stance* on your right leg, and execute a *left low block*

4A

B

3

B

5

Continued

with the knife hand. (6) Step forward with your right in the direction of I, assuming a *back stance* on your left leg, and execute a *right low block* with the knife hand. (7) Turning counterclockwise, place your left foot forward on line L2, assuming a *tiger stance* on your right leg, and execute a *right inward middle block* with the heel of your palm, placing your left fist below your right elbow, palm side down, (8) then, immediately execute a *right back fist* strike by pivoting your arm at the elbow, and maintaining the same stance. (9) Pivot clockwise on the ball of your left foot, and extend your right foot on line R2, assuming a *tiger stance* on your left leg, and execute a *left inward middle block* with the heel of your palm, placing your right fist below your left elbow, palm down, (10) then, immediately, execute a *left back fist* strike, by pivoting your right arm at the elbow, and maintaining the same stance. (11) Turn counterclockwise to face in the direction of I, bringing your left foot adjacent to your right, and cup your left fist in your right palm, positioning them before your chest.

6

9

7

8

10

11

Continued

(12A) Step forward with your left foot in the direction of I, assuming a *left extended forward stance,* and simultaneously, execute a *right reverse low block,* and a *left outward middle block,* then (12B) simultaneously, execute from the same stance a *right low block,* and a *left outward middle block.* (13A) Step forward with your right foot in the direction of I, assuming a *right extended forward stance,* and simultaneously, execute a *left reverse low block,* and *right outward middle block,* then (13B) simultaneously, execute from the same stance, a *right low block,* and a *left outward middle block.* (14) Pivot counterclockwise on the ball of your right foot to face R3, and extend your left foot on line R3, assuming a *left extended forward stance,* and execute an *outward double middle block.* (15A) Execute a *right knee strike,* then (15B) leap forward onto your right foot, and bring your left up behind your right, assuming a *cross legged stance,* and execute a *double*

12A

13B

14

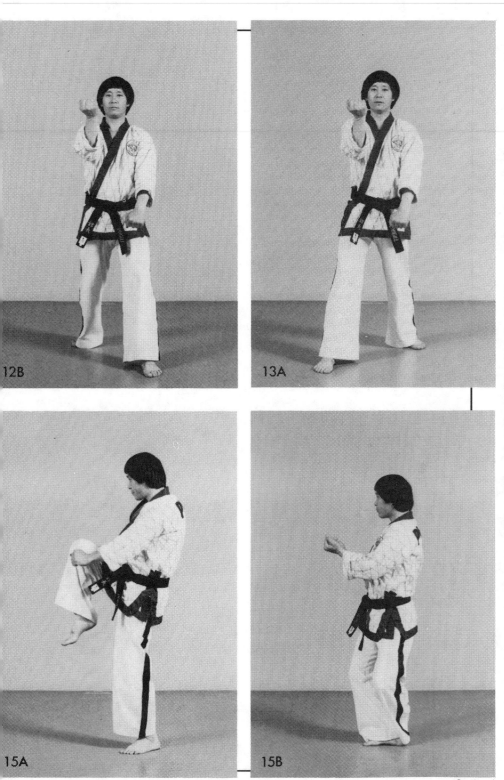

12B

13A

15A

15B

Continued

uppercut to the middle. (16) Extend your left foot back behind you, and assume a *right extended forward stance,* and execute a *low cross block.* (17) Pivot counterclockwise on the ball of your left foot and step forward with your right on line L3, assuming a *right extended forward stance,* and execute an *outward double block.* (18A) Execute a *left knee strike,* and (18B) leap forward onto your left foot, assuming a *cross legged stance,* and execute a *double uppercut* to the middle. (19) Extend your foot back behind you, assuming a *left extended forward stance,* and exeucte a *low cross block.* (20) Turn counterclockwise and step forward toward G with your left foot, assuming a *left forward stance,* and execute a *left backfist strike* to the side of the head. (21A) Execute a *right crescent kick,* then slap the arch of your right foot, with your left palm at its highest point. Allow your momentum to turn your body sideways, so

16

18B

19

17

18A

FRONT
VIEW

20

SIDE
VIEW

21A

Continued

that you may (21B) bring your right foot down into a *horse stance,* with your right shoulder facing in the direction of G, and execute a *right elbow strike,* slapping the contact area with your left palm. (22) Turn clockwise to face in the direction of G, assuming a *right forward stance,* and execute a *right backfist* strike. (23) Execute a *left crescent kick,* slapping the arch of your left foot with your right palm, and (23B) step sideways into a *horse stance* with your left shoulder facing in the direction of G, and execute a *left elbow strike,* slapping with your right palm. (24) Keeping the same stance, execute a *left outward middle block* in the direction of G. (25) With the left knife hand still extended, clench it into a fist, then pivot counterclockwise on the ball of your left foot into another *horse stance* with your right shoulder facing in the direction of G, and execute a *right side punch* in the direction of G, and yell. (26) Pivot counterclockwise on the ball of your right foot to face in the direction of I, assuming the *ready stance.*

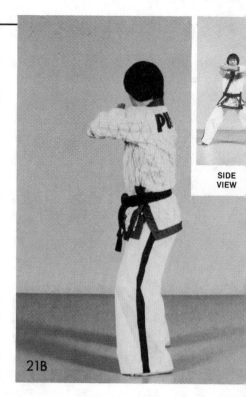

SIDE VIEW

21B

SIDE VIEW

23B

24

FRONT VIEW

FRONT
VIEW

SIDE
VIEW

22

23A

SIDE
VIEW

25

26

Chapter Nine

GON

his last group of Taegeuk actions is guided by the principle called *gon* which is defined as the quality of being receptive. Its metaphysic is pure *yang,* and it is symbolized by the earth, providing the substance into which the heavenly light and energy of keon enters to produce physical forms.

Taegeuk eight jang is intended as a summation and a review of all the previous forms for the student on his way to attaining the rank of black belt. Those of the brown belt rank are required to be proficient in this as well as the preceding forms.

TAEGEUK EIGHT JANG
AT A GLANCE

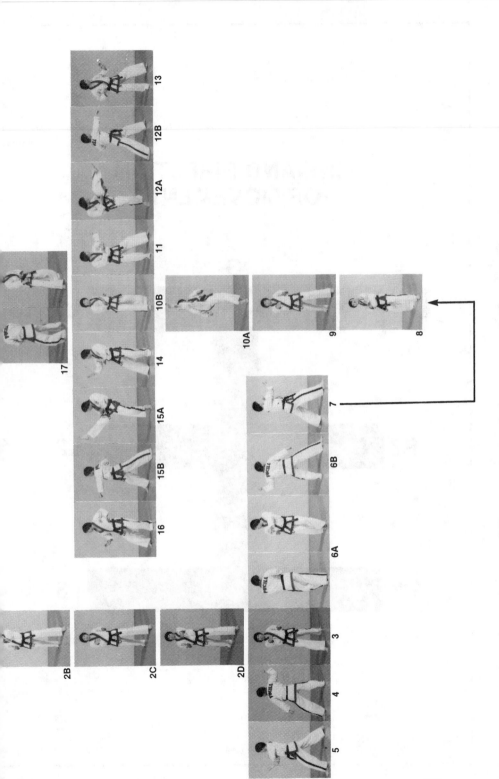

LINE AND DIRECTION
OF MOVEMENT

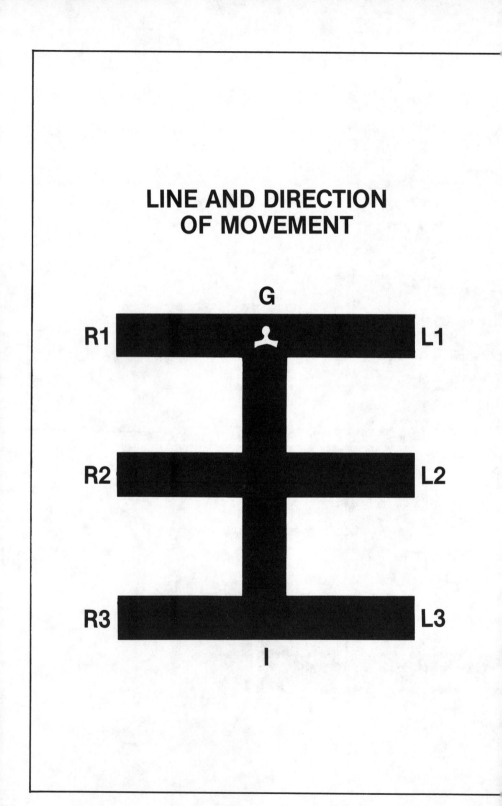

Ready
Stance

TAEGEUK EIGHT JANG

From the *ready stance,* (1A) step forward with your left foot in the direction of I, assuming a *back stance* on your right leg, and execute an *upward*

1A

Continued

1B

middle block and immediately (1B) assume a *left extended forward stance,* and execute a *right reverse front punch* to the middle. (2A) Execute a *right jumping front kick* followed by a left *jumping front kick,* and yell. Then, (2B) step forward with your left foot in the direction of I, assuming a *left extended forward stance,* and execute a *left inward middle block.* (2C) Then, execute a *right reverse front punch* to the middle from the same stance, followed by (2D) a *left front punch* to the middle from the same stance. (3) Step forward with your right foot in the direction of I, assuming a *right extended forward stance,* and execute a *right front punch* to the middle.

2C

2A

2B

2D

3

155 Continued

(4) Pivot counterclockwise on the ball of your right foot, swinging your left foot around behind you to step in the direction of R3, assuming a *right extended forward stance,* turning your head to look in the direction of R3, and execute a simultaneous *left low block* and a *right outward middle block.* (5) Pivot counterclockwise on the ball of your right foot, to face in the direction of R3, and step forward with your left foot, assuming a *left extended forward stance,* then pull your left fist in toward your right shoulder while simultaneously executing a *right uppercut* slowly. (6A) Pivot clockwise on the ball of your right foot to face in the direction of G. Looking in the direction of L3, cross your left foot in front of your right, assuming a *cross legged stance,* and bring your right fist to chest level, and your left fist to stomach level, then (6B) step toward L3 with your right foot, assuming a *left extended forward stance,* and execute a simultaneous *right low block* and a *left outward middle block.* (7) Pivot clockwise on the ball of your left foot and step forward with your right on L3, assuming a *right extended forward stance,* and simultaneously pull your right fist to your left shoulder and execute a *left uppercut* slowly. (8) Pivot counterclockwise on the ball of your left foot to face in the direction of I, and step back with your right foot in the direction of G, assuming a *back stance* on your right foot, and execute a *left outward middle block* with your knife

4

6B

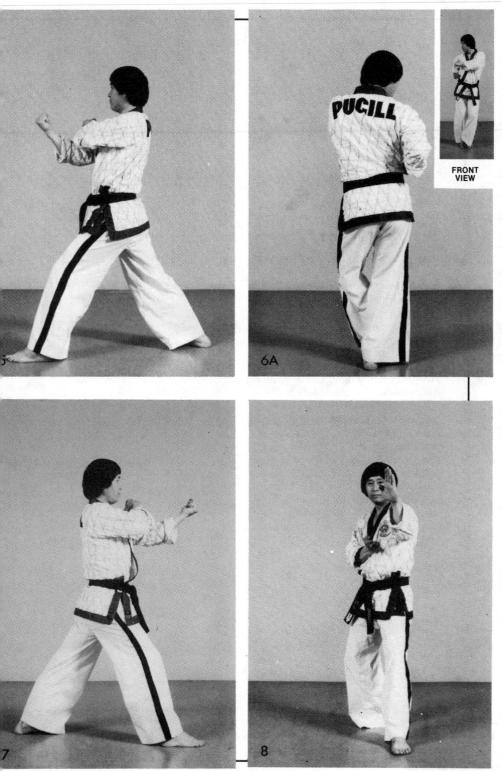

FRONT
VIEW

6A

7

8

157 Continued

hand. (9) Step forward with your left foot in the direction of I, assuming a *left extended forward stance,* and execute a *right reverse front punch.* (10A) Execute a *right front kick.* (10B) Return your right leg to its original position, then step backward with your left toward G, assuming a *tiger stance* on your left leg, and execute a *right downward middle block* with the heel of your palm. (11) Turn counterclockwise to face L2, and step forward with your left foot on L2, assuming a *tiger stance* on your right leg, and execute a *left outward middle block* with the knife hand. (12A) Execute a *left front kick,* then (12B) step forward with your left foot on L2, assuming a *left extended forward stance,* and execute a *right reverse*

10A

10B

2A

12B

Continued

13

front punch. (13) Keeping your right foot planted, shift back into a *tiger stance* on your right foot, and execute a *left downward middle block* with the heel of your palm. (14) Pivot clockwise on the ball of your right foot, and step forward with your right foot on R2, assuming a *tiger stance* on your right leg, and execute a *right outward middle block* with the knife hand. (15A) Execute a *right front kick,* then (15B) step forward with your right foot on R2, assuming a *right extended forward stance,* and execute a *left front punch.* (16) Keeping your left foot planted, shift back into a *tiger stance* on your left leg, and execute a *right downward middle block* with the heel of your palm. (17) Pivot clockwise on the ball of your left foot, and step forward with your right foot in the direction of G, assuming a *back stance* on your left leg, and execute a *right low block* with your left fist across your waist.

15B

14

15A

16

17

FRONT
VIEW

Continued

FRONT
VIEW

(18A) Execute a *left front kick,* and then (18B) a *right jumping front kick* while your left is still in the air. Then (18C) step down toward G, assuming a *right extended forward stance,* and execute a *right inward middle block,* and then (18D) a *left reverse front punch* from the same stance, and yell. (19) Pivot counterclockwise on the ball of your right foot, and step forward on L1 with your left, assuming a *back stance* on your right leg, and execute a *left outward middle block* with the knife hand. (20) Step forward with your left foot on L1, assuming a *left extended forward stance,* and execute a *right reverse*

18A

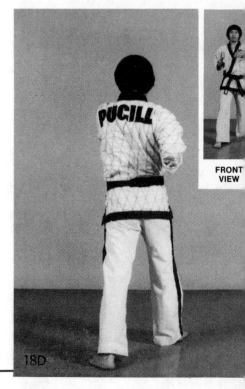

FRONT
VIEW

18D

FRONT
VIEW

FRONT
VIEW

18B

18C

9

20

Continued

elbow strike. (21A) Then, execute a *right reverse backfist strike* from the same stance, (21B) and then a *left front punch* from the same stance. (22) Pivot clockwise on the ball of your left foot, and step forward with your right foot on R1, assuming a *back stance* on your left leg, and execute a *right outward middle block* with the knife hand. (23) Step forward with your right foot on R1, assuming a *right extended forward stance,* and execute a *left reverse elbow strike.* (24A) Then, execute a *left reverse back fist strike* from the same stance, (24B) and then a *right front punch* from the same stance. (25) Turn to face in the direction of I, and bring your left foot adjacent to your right, assuming the *ready stance.*

21A

23

24A

21B

22

24B

25

End

Chapter Ten

KORYO

K *oryo* is the name of the Korean dynasty dated between the years 918 and 1392, from which the country, Korea derived its name—a designation which also implies the origination of a national character and identity.

The people of this dynasty successfully defended their homeland from the Mongolian imperialism to which much of Asia had succumbed.

This form, therefore, represents the cultivation of a strong conviction, and an unyielding spirit.

Black belts of the first degree are required to be proficient in this as well as the previous forms.

KORYO AT A GLANCE

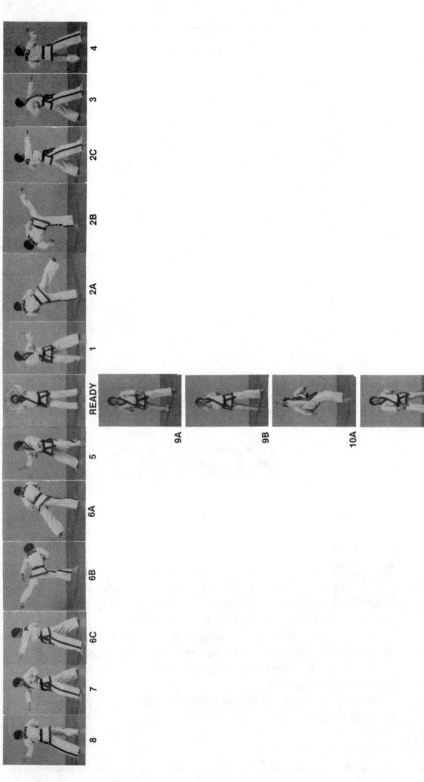

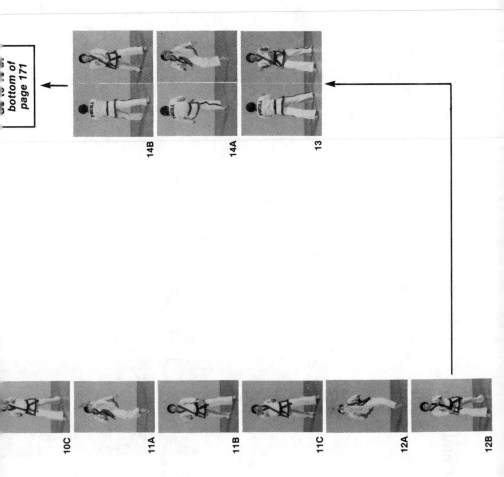

Go to 14 at bottom of page 171

14B

14A

13

10C

11A

11B

11C

12A

12B

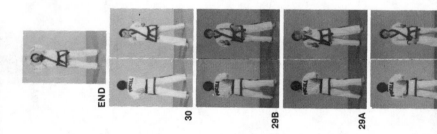

END

30

29B

29A

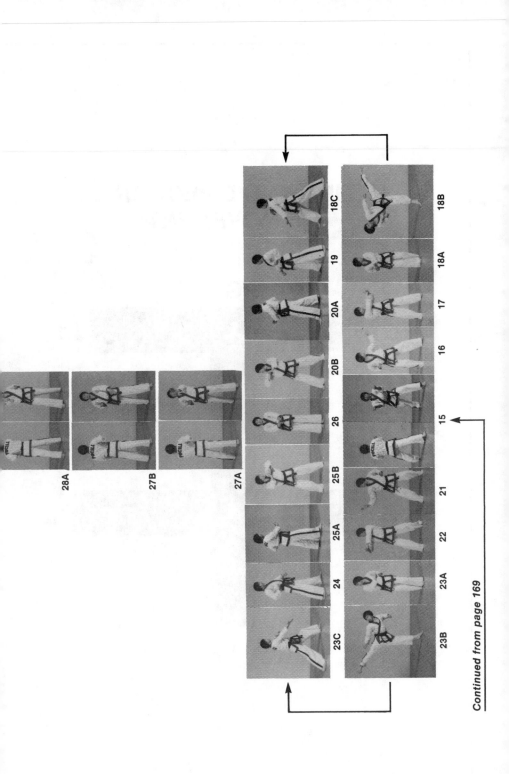

Continued from page 169

LINE AND DIRECTION
OF MOVEMENT

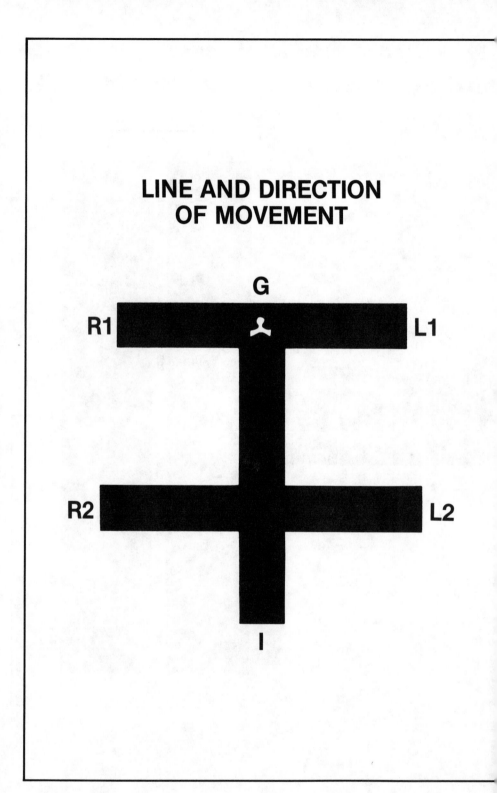

Ready
Stance

KORYO

Assume the *ready stance* by bringing both hands up in front of your chin, palms facing forward. (1) Turn to the left, and extend your left foot forward on line L1, assuming a *back stance* on your right leg, and execute a *left outward middle block* with the knife hand, your right knife hand in the palm up

1

Continued

2A

position at your abdomen. (2A) Pivoting on your left foot, execute a *low right side kick* in the direction of L1, and immediately (2B) execute a *side kick* with the same leg in the direction of L1, and (2C) step down with your right foot on line L1, assuming a *right extended forward stance,* and execute a *right knife hand strike* to the opponent's neck on his right side. (3) Then, from the same stance, execute a *left reverse front punch* to the middle. (4) Keeping your right foot in the same position, slide your left foot forward on line L1, assuming a *back stance* on your left leg, and execute a *right inward middle block* with the ulna side of the wrist. (5) Pivot clockwise on the ball of your right foot to face in the direction of R1, and step forward with your right on R1, assuming a *back stance* on your left leg, and execute a *right outward middle block* with the knife hand, with your left knife hand in the palm up position at your abdomen.

3

2B

2C

4

5

Continued

(6A) Pivoting on your right foot, execute a *low left side kick* in the direction of R1, and immediately (6B) execute a *high side kick* with the same leg in the direction of R1, and (6C) step down with your left foot on line R1, assuming a *left extended forward stance*, and execute a *left knife hand strike* to the opponent's neck on his left side. (7) From the same stance, execute a *right reverse front punch* to the middle. (8) Slide your right foot forward along line R1, assuming a *back stance* on your right leg, and execute a *left inward middle block* with the ulna side of the wrist. (9A) Pivot counterclockwise on the ball of your right foot, and move your left foot one step forward in the direction of I, assuming a *left extended forward stance,* and execute a *left low block* with the knife

6A

7

6B

6C

8

9A

Continued

9B

hand. (9B) From the same stance, execute a *right reverse open hand thrust* using the edge of your hand between the index finger and thumb as the striking area. (10A) Execute a *right front kick,* and (10B) drop the right foot forward toward I, assuming a *right extended forward stance,* and execute a *right low block* with the knife hand, and (10C) from the same stance, execute a *left reverse open hand thrust.* (11A) Keeping the left hand in the same position, execute a *right front kick,* and (11B) drop your left foot one step forward toward I, assuming a *left extended forward stance,* and execute *left low block* with the knife hand, and

10C

10A

10B

11A

11B

Continued

11C

(11C) from the same stance, execute a *right reverse open hand strike.* (12A) Keeping the right hand in the same position, execute a *right front kick,* and (12B) drop your right foot one step forward toward I, assuming a *right extended forward stance,* and execute a *knee break* by grabbing your opponent's heel in your right palm facing up at waist level, and pulling upward to your chest, while at the same time pushing downward on his knee with your left palm facing down from your chest to your waist level. (13) Pivot clockwise on the ball of your right foot to face in the direction of G, assuming a *right extended forward stance,* and execute an *outward middle block* with the thumb sides of the wrists. (14A) Execute a *left front kick,* and (14B) drop the left foot one step forward toward G, assuming a *left extended forward stance,* and execute a *knee break,* grabbing the heel with the left hand, pushing down on the knee with

FRONT VIEW

13

2A

12B

4A

FRONT
VIEW

14B

FRONT
VIEW

Continued

FRONT
VIEW

the right hand. (15) Keeping the right foot fixed, slide the left up in the direction of G, assuming a *left forward stance,* and execute an *outward double middle block* with the thumb sides of the wrist. (16) Pivot clockwise on the ball of your left foot to face in the direction of L2, but bring your right foot back behind you to the line R2, assuming a *horse stance,* and execute a *left outward middle block* with the knife hand in the direction of L2. (17) Keeping the same stance, execute a *right hook punch* to the middle across your body in the direction of L2, slapping your left palm to the fist. (18A) Cross your right foot in front of your left, assuming a *cross legged stance,* and (18B) execute a *left side kick* in the direction of L2, and (18C) drop your left foot forward on line L2, and turn counterclockwise to face in the direction of R2, assuming a *right extended forward stance,* and execute a left *low reverse spear thrust* palm up, simultaneously bringing your right hand across your chest ot the left

15

18A

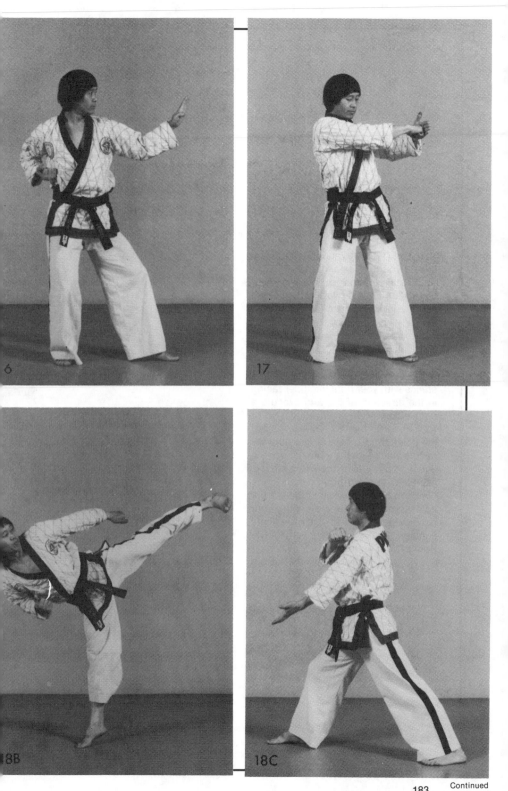

16

17

18B

18C

183 Continued

19

shoulder. (19) shift your right foot back toward your left, assuming a *right forward stance,* and execute a *right block.* (20A) Step forward with your left foot in the direction of R2, assuming a *left forward stance,* and execute a *left inward middle block* with the heel of your palm. (20B) Swing your right foot around, turning counterclockwise, and place it on line R2, assuming a *horse stance* with your right shoulder facing in the direction of R2, and execute a *right elbow strike* in the direction of R2, supporting your right fist in your left palm. (21) Execute a *right outward middle block* with the knife hand in the direction of R2 from the same stance. (22) Execute a *left hook punch* in the direction of R2 by hooking the left fist across your body, and slapping your right palm to the left fist to indicate contact. (23A) Cross your left foot in front of your right along R2, assuming

21

20A

20B

2

23A

Continued

a *cross legged stance,* then (23B) execute a *right side kick* in the direction of R2. (23C) Drop your right foot down on line R2, and turn your body counterclockwise to face in the direction of L2, assuming a *left extended forward stance,* and execute a *right low reverse spear thrust* palm up. (24) Shift your left foot back toward your right, assuming a *left forward stance,* and execute a *left low block.* (25A) Step forward with your right assuming a *right forward stance,* and execute a *right inward middle block.* (25B) Swing your left foot around, turning clockwise, and place it on line L2, assuming a *horse stance,* and execute a *left elbow strike* in the direction of L2. (26) Slide your right foot over, and place it adjacent to your left, slowly raising both hands over your head, then execute a low hammerfist strike, by bringing both hands down slowly. (27A) Pivot counterclockwise on the ball of your right foot, and step forward with your left in the direction of G, assuming a *left extended forward stance,* and ex-

23B

25A

25B

FRONT
VIEW

Continued

ecute a *left outward knife hand strike,* and (27B) execute a *left low block* with the knife hand from the same stance. (28A) Step forward with your right foot in the direction of G, assuming a *right extended forward stance,* and execute a *right inward knife hand strike,* then (28B) execute a *right low block* with the knife hand from the same stance. (29A) Step forward with your left foot in the direction of G, assuming a *left extended forward stance,* and execute a *left inward knife hand strike,* then (29B) execute a *left low block* with the knife hand from the same stance. (30) Step forward with your right foot in the direction of G, assuming a *right extended forward stance,* and execute a *right open hand thrust* to the throat. (31) Pivot counterclockwise on the ball of your right foot to face in the direction of I, shifting your left foot back to a position adjacent your right foot, shoulder width apart, assuming your original *ready stance* by bringing both hands up in front of your chin, palms facing forward.

FRONT VIEW

27B

FRONT VIEW

29A

FRONT VIEW

29B

FRONT VIEW

28A

FRONT VIEW

28B

FRONT VIEW

30

31

End

Chapter Eleven

KEUMGANG

 eumgang means hardness. In addition, the name has two connotations applicable to tae kwon do: one poetic, and the other spiritual. The Korean people have named the most beautiful mountain in their land Keumgang-san; and the hardest substance, the diamond, they have called *keumgang-seok*. These dual qualities of hardness and beauty are therefore associated with the name. Buddhist thought also professes a concept of hardness which is that quality of spirit impervious to mortal agony; it is the capacity to shun one's physical suffering.

This form, in turn, being called keumgang, is intended to fuse these qualities with one's martial skills, and in so doing, grace them with virtue.

Black belts of the second degree are required to be proficient in this and all previous forms.

KEUMGANG AT A GLANCE

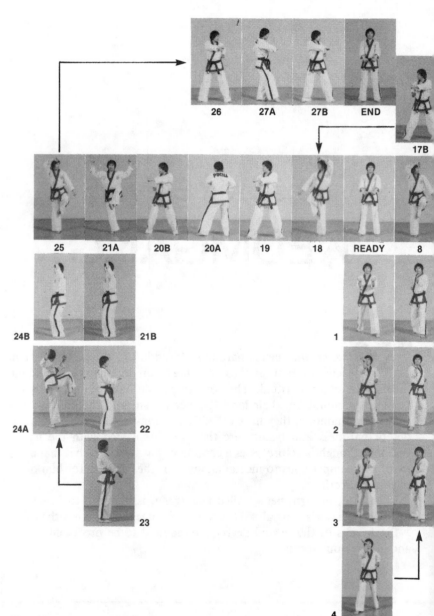

26   27A   27B   END

17B

25   21A   20B   20A   19   18   READY   8

24B   21B   1

24A   22   2

23   3

4

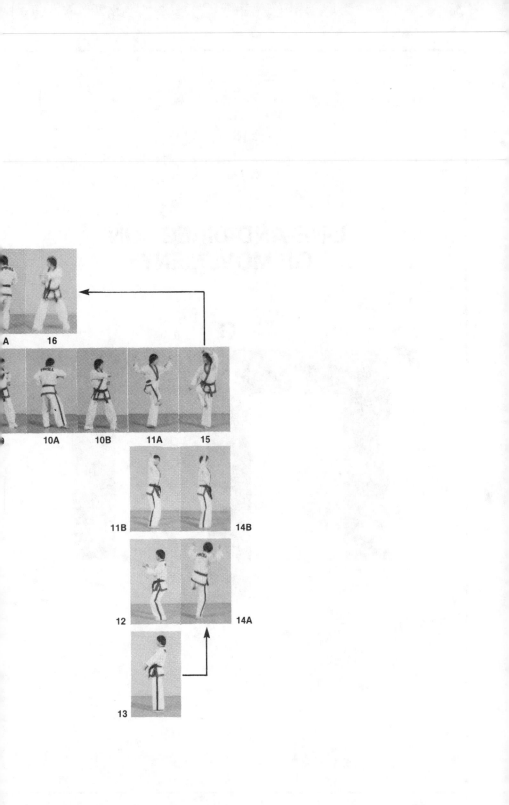

A   16

10A   10B   11A   15

11B   14B

12   14A

13

LINE AND DIRECTION
OF MOVEMENT

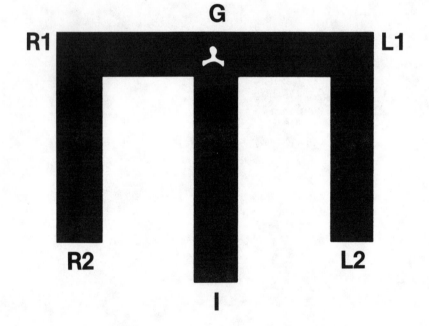

Ready Stance

KEUMGANG

From the *ready stance,* (1) step forward with your left foot in the direction of I, assuming a *left extended forward stance,* and execute an *outward*

I

double middle block. (2) Step forward with your right foot in the direction of I, assuming a *right extended forward stance,* and execute a *right high palm heel strike.* (3) Step forward with your left foot in the direction of I, assuming a *left extended forward stance,* and execute a *left high palm heel strike.* (4) Step forward with your right foot in the direction of I, assuming a *right extended forward stance,* and execute a *right high palm heel strike.* (5) Step backward with your right foot in the direction of G, assuming a *back stance* on your right leg, and execute a *left inward middle block* with the knife hand. (6) Step backward with your left foot in the direction of G, assuming a *back stance* on your left leg, and execute a *right inward middle block* with the knife hand. (7) Step backward with your right foot in the direction of G, assuming a *back stance* on your right leg, and execute a *left inward middle block* with the knife hand. (8) Assume

2

5

6

3

4

7

8

Continued

a *crane stance* on your right leg, turning your head to look in the direction of L1, and execute simultaneously, a *right high block,* and a *left low block.* (9) Step to the left side, dropping your left foot on line L1, assuming a *horse stance,* and execute a *right hook punch.* (10A) Pivot counterclockwise in a complete circle on the ball of your left foot, to end with your right foot close to your left, but not touching, then (10B) step to the side with your left foot in the direction of L1, assuming a *horse stance,* and execute a *right hook punch.* (11A) Pivot counterclockwise on the ball of your left foot, raising your right knee up to waist level, and your fists up to head level, then (11B) stomp your right foot down in the direction of L2, assuming a *horse stance,* and execute a *double block.* (12) Pivot clockwise on the ball of your right foot, swinging your left foot around to step in the direction of L2, assuming a *horse stance,* and execute a *double outward middle block.* (13)

9

11A

11B

10A

10B

12

13

Continued

Shift your left foot closer to your right foot, and execute a *double low block.* (14) Pivot clockwise on the ball of your right foot, raising both fists up to head level, and your knee up to waist level, then (14A) stomp your left foot down in the direction of L1, assuming a *horse stance,* and execute a *double high block.* (15) Pivot clockwise on the ball of your left foot so that your right side faces in the direction of R1, assuming a *crane stance* on your left leg, and execute simultaneously, a *left high block* and a *right low block.* (16) Step to the right side in the direction of R1, assuming a *horse stance,* and execute a *left hook punch.* (17A) Pivot clockwise in a complete circle on the ball of your right foot to end with your left foot close to your right but not touching, then (17B) step sideways with your right foot in the direction of R1, assuming a *horse stance,* and execute a *left hook punch.* (18) Assume a *crane stance* on your left leg, and execute simultaneously, a *left high block* and a

14A

16

17A

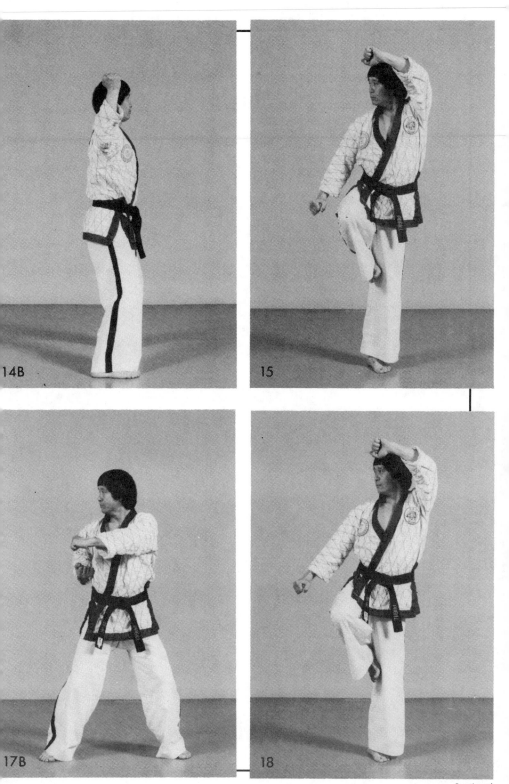

14B

15

17B

18

Continued

right low block. (19) Step sideways with your right foot in the direction of R1, assuming a *horse stance,* and execute a *left hook punch.* (20A) Pivot clockwise in a complete circle on the ball of your right foot to end with your left foot close to your right but not touching, (20B) step sideways with your right foot in the direction of R1, assuming a *horse stance,* and execute a *left hook punch.* (21A) Pivot clockwise on the ball of your right foot, raising your fists up to head level, and your knee up to waist level, then (21B) stomp your left foot down in the direction of R2, assuming a *horse stance,* and execute a *double high block.* (22) Pivot counterclockwise on the ball of your left foot, swinging your right around to step in the direction of R2, assuming a *horse stance,* and execute a *double outward middle block.* (23) Bring your right foot in closer to your left, and execute a *low*

19

21A

21B

20A

20B

22

23

Continued

double block. (24A) Pivot counter-clockwise on the ball of your left foot, raising your fists above your head level, and your right knee up to waist level, then (24B) stomp your right foot down in the direction of R1, assuming a *horse stance,* and execute a *double high block.* (25) Pivot counterclock-wise on the ball of your right foot, assuming a *crane stance,* and execute simultaneously, a *right high block,* and a *left low block.* (26) Step sideways with your left foot in the direction of L1, assuming a *horse stance*, and execute a *right hook punch.* (27A) Pivot counterclockwise in a complete circle on the ball of your left foot, to end with your right foot close to your left, but not touching, then (27B) step sideways with your left foot in the direction of L1, assuming a *horse stance,* and execute a *right hook punch.* (28) Pull in your left foot adjacent to your right, assuming the *ready stance,* eyes forward looking in the direction of I.

24A

26

27A

24B

25

27B

28

End

Chapter Twelve

TAEBAEK

 aebaek was the name of a region of Korea where, according to legend, the Korean nation was founded more than 4,300 years ago. This region is now Mount Baekdoo, but the word *tae-baek*, still identifies the source of Korea, and the majesty of Mount Baekdoo, and so it is associated with light, this being the source of life, and sanctity because the mountain is close to perfection.

This form is named taeback because it is meant to portray these abstract qualities. Black belts of the third degree are required to be proficient in this form as well as the preceding forms.

4C   4B   4A   3   READY   1

TAEBAEK
AT A GLANCE

5

6A

6B

7A

7B

8A

13B   13A   12   11   10   9   8B   14

2A 2B 2C

END

26C 26B 26A 25 22 23 24A 24B 24C

21B

21A

20

19

15 16 17 18A 18B

LINE AND DIRECTION
OF MOVEMENT

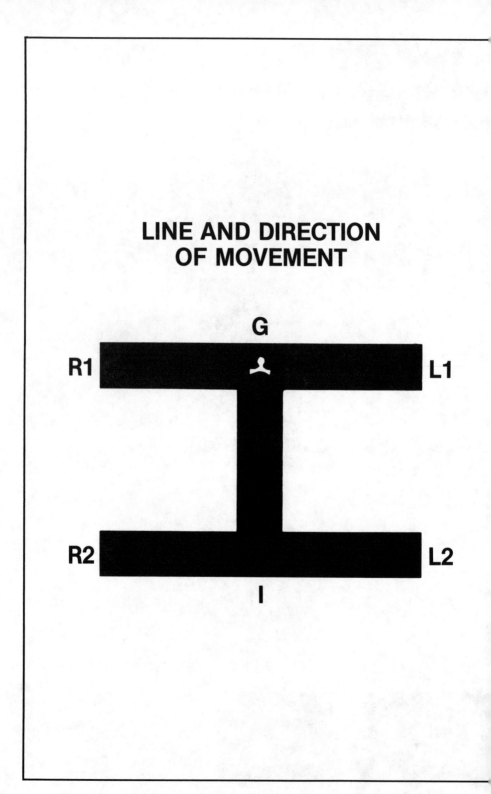

Ready Stance

TAEBAEK

From the *ready stance,* (1) turn counterclockwise and step forward with your left foot on line L1, assuming a *tiger stance* on your right leg, and execute a *double low block* with the

1

Continued

2A

knife hands. (2A) Execute a *right front kick,* and (2B) step forward with your right foot on line L1, assuming a *right extended forward stance,* and execute a *right front punch* to the middle, and (2C) execute a *left reverse front punch* to the middle from the same stance. (3) Pivot counterclockwise on the ball of your left foot, and step forward with your right foot on line R1, assuming a *tiger stance,* on your left leg, and execute a *double low block* with the knife hands. (4A) Execute a *left front kick,* and (4B) step forward with your left foot on line R1, assuming a *left extended forward stance,* and execute a *left front punch* to the

3

2B

2C

4A

4B

Continued

4C

middle, and then (4C) execute a *right reverse front punch* to the middle from the same stance. (5) Pivot counterclockwise on the ball of your right foot, and step forward with your left foot toward I, assuming a *left extended forward stance,* and execute a simultaneous *left high block* and a *right inward knife hand strike* to the neck. (6A) Execute a *right downward middle block* with the heel of your palm slowly, then (6B) step forward with your right foot toward I, assuming a *right extended forward stance,* and execute a *left reverse punch* to the middle. (7A) Execute a *left downward middle block* with the heel of your palm slowly, then (7B) step forward with your left foot toward I, assuming a *left extended forward stance,* and execute a *right reverse front punch* to the middle.

6B

5

6A

7A

7B

Continued

(8A) Execute a *right downward middle block* with the heel of your palm slowly, then (8B) step forward with your right foot toward I, assuming a *right extended forward stance,* and execute a *left reverse front punch* to the middle. (9) Pivot counterclockwise on the ball of your right foot, and step forward on line R2, assuming a *back stance* on your right leg and execute a simultaneous *left outward middle block* and a *right high block.* (10) Pull your left fist to your right shoulder, and execute a *right uppercut* from the same stance. (11) Execute a *left side punch* from the same stance. (12) Lift your left foot up into a *crane stance* on your right leg, then (13A) execute a *left side kick,* and a *left side punch*

8A

10

11

8B

9

2

13A

Continued

simultaneously. (13B) Step down with your left foot on line R2, assuming a *left extended forward stance,* and execute a *right reverse elbow strike.* (14) Bring your left foot adjacent to your right, facing in the direction of G, then immediately, step to the right with your right foot on line L2, assuming a *back stance* on your left leg, and execute a simultaneous *left high block* and *right outward middle block.* (15) Pull your right fist to your left shoulder, and execute a *left uppercut* from the same stance. (16) Execute a *right side punch* from the same stance. (17) Raise your right foot into a *crane stance* on your left leg, then (18A) execute a *right side kick* and a *right side punch* simultaneously, then (18B) step down with your right foot on line R2, assuming a *right extended forward stance,* and execute a

13B

16

17

14

15

18A

18B

219 Continued

left reverse elbow strike. (19) Bring your right foot to your left, then step with your left toward G, assuming a *back stance* on your right leg, and execute *right outward middle block* with the knife hand. (20) Step forward with your right foot toward G, assuming a *right extended forward stance,* and execute a *right spear thrust* to the middle. (21A) Pivot by twisting your body counterclockwise, and turn your extended spear hand upside down, then (21B) pivot clockwise on the ball of your right foot and swing your left foot around toward G, assuming a *back stance* on your right leg, and execute a *left back fist strike.* (22) Step toward G with your right foot, assuming a *right extended forward stance,* and execute a *right front punch* to the middle. (23) Pivot counterclockwise on the ball of your right foot, and step forward with your left foot on line L1, assuming a *left extended forward stance* and execute a simultaneous *left low block and right outward middle block.* (24A) Execute a *right front*

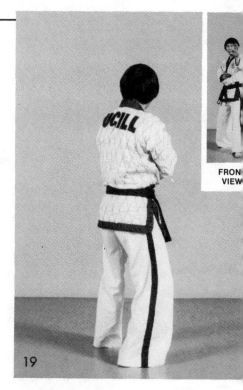

FRONT VIEW

19

FRONT VIEW

21B

22

FRONT VIEW

FRONT
VIEW

SIDE
VIEW

20

21A

23

24A

Continued

kick, and (24B) step forward with your right foot on line L1, assuming a *right extended forward stance,* and execute a *right front punch* to the middle, then (24C) execute a *left reverse front punch* to the middle from the same stance. (25) Pivot clockwise on the ball of your left foot, and step forward with your right foot on line R1, assuming a *right extended forward stance,* and execute a simultaneous *right low block* and a *left outward middle block.* (26A) Execute a *left front kick,* and (26B) step forward with your left foot on line R1, assuming a *left extended forward stance,* and execute a *left front punch* to the middle, then (26C) execute a *right reverse front punch* to the middle from the same stance. (27) Pivot counterclockwise on the ball of your right foot, bringing your left foot adjacent to your right, facing in the direction of I, and assume the *ready stance.*

24B

26A

26B

24C

25

26C

27